Praise for *Talking to Depression*

"This book recognizes the power of altruism in healing, and the capacities of a depressed person to herself be a healer for others. . . . Strauss not only suggests how we can be a good friend to a friend who is depressed, but she provides us instructions on *how* to be a good friend. [*Talking to Depression* is] a really important tool for knowing how to relate and how to connect when people in your life are struggling with depression."   —Jo Cohen Hamilton, Ph.D., Professor of Counseling and Human Services at Kutztown University

"*Talking to Depression* is a war chest of tools to aid our understanding of something that defies understand͟ ͟ ͟ ͟ ͟ first-hand. . . . In an ideal world [this͟ ͟ ͟ ͟ ͟ ext best thing would be that it find͟ ͟ ͟ ͟ ͟ ry. Perhaps, in the right hands, this͟ ͟ ͟ ͟ ͟
     —Christine B. Sr͟ ͟ ͟ ͟ ͟ nc.
     (Survivors or ͟ ͟ ͟ ͟ ͟ de)

"Ms. Strauss has created a wonderfully helpful book for all of us. An excellent manual for the day-to-day interaction with the depressed person. This book would be a wonderful addition to anyone's library that unfortunately will get excellent use!"   —Peter A. Schwartz, M.D.

"It is an essential read for the layperson that does not understand the experience of depression and wants to help a friend or family member through it . . . practical ideas, common sense guidelines and clear explanations that can make a difference in the lives of those with depression."   —Marta C. Peck, Executive Director of the Mental Health Association of Reading, PA, and Berks County

continued . . .

"This book is about what the person suffering from depression needs to hear and, even more importantly, about what that person should *not* hear. . . . Strauss doesn't just give the persons with depression a chance to get the daily support they need, she gives the people who love them a way to feel renewed in their own lives. I found it enlightening, inspiring, and enormously instructive."

—Nancy Wolter Brooks, speech pathologist, and health, rehabilitation, and social work professional

"This magical book . . . makes numerous practical, valuable, and doable suggestions. It shows family and friends how to make a difference. With this guide, we can help the people we know who are struggling with this disease, and we can help ourselves. I couldn't recommend this book more strongly."

—Catherine M. Schultz, School Counselor, Reading High School

"I can't say enough about Claudia Strauss's *Talking to Depression*. This is definitely a guide that is needed. I've never seen anything that addresses friends and family in this way—and so thoroughly, so compassionately, yet so simply. What a contribution to the field!"

—Michelle L. Hostetter, Psy.D., Clinical Psychologist

Talking
to
Anxiety

Simple Ways to
Support Someone in Your Life
Who Suffers from Anxiety

CLAUDIA J. STRAUSS

WITH A FOREWORD BY
JEANNE ALBRONDA HEATON, PH.D.

New American Library

New American Library
Published by New American Library, a division of
Penguin Group (USA) Inc., 375 Hudson Street,
New York, New York 10014, USA
Penguin Group (Canada), 10 Alcorn Avenue, Toronto,
Ontario M4V 3B2, Canada (a division of Pearson Penguin Canada Inc.)
Penguin Books Ltd., 80 Strand, London WC2R 0RL, England
Penguin Ireland, 25 St. Stephen's Green, Dublin 2,
Ireland (a division of Penguin Books Ltd.)
Penguin Group (Australia), 250 Camberwell Road, Camberwell, Victoria 3124,
Australia (a division of Pearson Australia Group Pty. Ltd.)
Penguin Books India Pvt. Ltd., 11 Community Centre, Panchsheel Park,
New Delhi – 110 017, India
Penguin Group (NZ), Cnr Airborne and Rosedale Roads, Albany,
Auckland 1310, New Zealand (a division of Pearson New Zealand Ltd.)
Penguin Books (South Africa) (Pty.) Ltd., 24 Sturdee Avenue,
Rosebank, Johannesburg 2196, South Africa

Penguin Books Ltd., Registered Offices:
80 Strand, London WC2R 0RL, England

First published by New American Library,
a division of Penguin Group (USA) Inc.

First Printing, December 2004
10   9   8   7   6   5   4   3   2   1

Copyright © Claudia J. Strauss, 2004
Foreword copyright © Jeanne Albronda Heaton, 2004
All rights reserved

 REGISTERED TRADEMARK—MARCA REGISTRADA

LIBRARY OF CONGRESS CATALOGING-IN-PUBLICATION DATA:

Strauss, Claudia J., 1952–
    Talking to anxiety : simple ways to support someone in your life who suffers from anxiety /
Claudia J. Strauss ; with a foreword by Jeanne Albronda Heaton.
        p.   cm.
    ISBN 0-451-21209-6 (trade pbk.)
    1. Anxiety—Popular works.   2. Anxiety—Patients—Family relationships.   I. Title.
RC531.S76   2004
616.85'22—dc22   2004015010

Set in Minion
Designed by Ginger Legato

Printed in the United States of America

To the three Nancys, who helped me hang on; to the
two Marilyns, who made me feel strong; to Michelle,
who always listened; to Marion, who believed in me;
to Ellen, who understood; to Catherine,
who never judged.

꒰꒱

To Howard and Ethel, who knew it was real; to both
Karens, who'd been there, too; to Hilde, who gave me
unqualified support and love; to Eva and Frank, who
always came; to my mother, who checked in daily.

꒰꒱

To Judy and Lotte, who would have made all the
difference, if only they could have been there.

꒰꒱

And to all those who live with a tearing at the heart
and mind, with the clawing of a demanding force,
that makes life so difficult for those they love.
I hope this book can help you help them.

Acknowledgments

I'd like to thank Jim Levine and Claire Zion for their belief in this book, and for encouraging me to take it on.

And I'd like to thank the usual suspects for reviewing the manuscript at various stages and for making wonderful suggestions, with special thanks to Marta Peck and Jo Cohen Hamilton for their careful reading through several incarnations.

I would particularly like to acknowledge the person who has been down in the trenches with me on this book, and that is Rose Hilliard, who has helped to make this book the best that it can be. It's a wonderful thing to feel a partnership with one's editor.

And it's a wonderful thing to develop a relationship with the person who takes on the Foreword. Thank you, Jeanne Albronda Heaton, for reading my manuscript and embracing it, and for your many invaluable suggestions.

My thanks to all the others who make up the NAL team, particularly Tracy Bernstein and Laura Cifelli who were involved in the editorial process, and Peter Ciccotto and Ginger Legato who, respectively, developed the cover and interior design, and made the book accessible and easy to read.

I am also grateful to Nanette Gartrell for generously allowing me to benefit from her experience (and written account) of the rare extreme reactions that can occur as side effects to medications among some people, and for reviewing what I'd written.

So many people have had an influence on this book, directly and indirectly; if you have touched my life or the lives of people I care about, that is likely reflected here in some way. I wish I could mention you all.

"A day of worry is more exhausting than a day of work."

∿ JOHN LUBBOCK

Contents

Foreword xiii
by Jeanne Albronda Heaton

Preface *xxi*

PART I—GETTING STARTED

Chapter One 5
An Overview of Anxiety: Frequently Asked Questions
Chapter Two 33
Help Is Available: Things to Know About Treatment
Chapter Three 47
What To Do First: Determining Your Role
Chapter Four 59
Seeing Through Their Eyes: What Anxiety Feels Like

PART II—WORDS MATTER

Chapter Five 69
Opening the Conversation: First Things to Say
Chapter Six 77
Words That Wobble: Giving It a Name
Chapter Seven 83
Words That Hurt: What Not to Say
Chapter Eight 93
Words That Help: What to Say

CONTENTS

Chapter Nine 101
Do's and Don'ts: A Helpful Reference
Chapter Ten 107
When They Ask Questions: How to Respond

PART III—ACTIONS MATTER

Chapter Eleven 121
Beyond Words: What Body Language Can Do
Chapter Twelve 127
Beyond Language: The Power of Silence
Chapter Thirteen 131
Triggers and Flashpoints: Making Their World Safe
Chapter Fourteen 145
Sources of Strength: Other Ways to Give

PART IV—LIVING DAY BY DAY

Chapter Fifteen 157
Seesawing Emotions: How to Respond
Chapter Sixteen 171
Situation by Situation: One Thing at a Time

PART V—KIDS AND TEENAGERS

Chapter Seventeen 191
Tips for Kids: When Someone Close to Them Suffers from Anxiety
Chapter Eighteen 207
What About Kids: When They Suffer from Anxiety Themselves

PART VI—TAKING CARE OF YOURSELF

Chapter Nineteen 225
Living with Stress: Keeping Yourself Whole

Afterword 233
Resources 237
How to Learn More: Finding Information and Support

Foreword

If you have gotten beyond the cover of this book, in all likelihood it's because you know how frustrating it is to deal with an anxious person. You wish you knew how to make a difference. Maybe you feel like you've done everything you thought would help and the situation hasn't improved. You'd like to figure out what to do next. Surely, you do NOT want to continue:

- Being afraid to say what you think because you don't want to make him worse
- Trying to coax her to leave the house
- Having to listen to him talk about everything that could go wrong
- Spending twelve hours in a car because an airplane terrifies her
- Being amazed that you can't convince him that he won't fail
- Feeling scared that maybe this time her fears of a heart attack are real
- Thinking it's crazy to keep telling him "you're not going crazy," all the while thinking, *but you are making me crazy!*

Rest assured, you're not alone. There are many family members, friends, coaches, teachers, religious advisors, and colleagues who realize they have an important role to play, but who also feel somewhat at a loss as to what to do and say. It's easy to feel stuck when you can't seem to find a way to reassure someone who is anxious.

Your choice to learn how to Talk to Anxiety has the potential to make both your life and someone else's much easier. As a therapist in practice for close to 30 years, I'm acutely aware of the importance of your role. First of all, most people suffering from anxiety never make it to therapy. And for those who do come for help, there are many hours between appointments where they rely on those close by for assistance and support. And not least importantly, your knowing what to do and say has the potential to alleviate some of your own discomfort of being around someone else's intense anxiety.

When people with anxiety problems know that someone close by can help, they feel calmer. They release some of the fear that leads them to avoid the most basic of life's activities and they begin building the coping skills that will actually provide the courage necessary to conquer the crippling feelings of anxiety that have left them sidelined.

WHEN ANXIETY BECOMES A THIEF

We are all programmed to respond to nerve-racking events. We know that even thinking about what could happen can lead us to react. Likewise, remembering something that happened years ago can sometimes make us feel those same emotions. When we are faced with this kind of stress our bodies release hormones that raise blood pressure, increase our heart rate, rush oxygen to the muscles and release sugar for quick energy. In mild forms anxiety makes us alert and attentive. It's a necessary signal that we need to pay attention and focus our efforts. Most of us use this burst of energy and sense of alertness to solve problems and get away from danger. That's a good thing.

You probably already know something about this basic "flight or fight" response. Essentially we all have the primitive physiology that allows us to deal with danger. Our basic chemistry has us wired to fight or run away. Fundamentally, the energy required to do battle or flee quickly is the physiology of anxiety—the racing heart, the fear, the increased blood pressure, the alertness, the dread.

Many people enjoy this intense state of arousal. They climb mountains, ride roller coasters, watch horror movies, race cars, tame wild animals, perform in front of large audiences. Doing these things under controlled conditions is often experienced as pleasurable. The key is under controlled conditions. The control that makes these feeling of anxiety acceptable (or even desirable) comes from the person choosing to participate, feeling prepared to handle the stress of the situation and most important, being able to anticipate the consequences of this circumstance. In fact, what we tell ourselves about our circumstances and feelings has a lot to do with how in control we feel.

But you are reading this book because the anxiety you have observed seems out of control and is causing problems for that person and others. Typically people notice symptoms or signs that there is a problem in one or more of four areas:

MOTOR:

- He never sits still
- She fidgets all the time (plays with her hair, fiddles with her pencils, cleans up constantly)

- He's always bouncing his leg and he hums
- She startles with any little thing

MOOD:

- He's tense
- She is apprehensive and worries all the time
- He expresses feelings of doom and gloom, always seems afraid of the worst
- She reports feeling depressed and irritable (depression is often a secondary symptom—we'll talk about that in a minute)

THOUGHT:

- He is always focused on what went wrong
- She worries about what will happen in the future
- He seems so distracted
- She is convinced she'll embarrass herself and end up feeling humiliated

PHYSIOLOGY:

- He complains of sweating, a dry mouth, shallow breathing, a rapid pulse
- She gets dizzy and feels nauseated
- He complains of chronic muscle tension
- She has high blood pressure, headaches, muscle weakness, and stomach problems, all consequences of stress, according to her doctor

You may be wondering what is causing the anxiety you observe. You may not know if what you observe is primary which means the anxiety is causing the problem(s), or secondary which means something else is causing the anxiety. For example, people can experience anxiety symptoms when they take cocaine, drink too much coffee or have a manic episode. In that case the symptoms are coming from the primary problem of substance abuse or some other mental health problem. You may also have noticed that the person you care about, like many other people who suffer from anxiety, also has trouble with depression. What is important for you to know now, is that you don't have to figure out which is primary or secondary in order to be helpful. Likewise, you don't need to know what's causing the problems you observe. But you do need to recognize that there is a problem before you can look for solutions.

Essentially, you know there is a problem if one or all of these 3 D's are present: **distress, disability**, and **duration**. You might ask yourself, "Is this anxiety causing me or the person I care about significant distress?" Or, "Is this anxiety causing significant suffering to this person or to others?" Likewise, you'll need to determine if the anxiety is interfering with his ability to work, to enjoy friends, family and activities. If his basic life tasks take a backseat to simply managing these intense and disruptive feelings, you know there is a problem. Most people are able to go back to their own level of functioning six to eight weeks following a disturbing event. However, if the anxiety you notice has gone on so long that it is now taking a significant toll on the health and wellbeing of a person in your life who is suffering, reading *Talking to Anxiety* will help you.

For most people, being overwhelmed with anxiety is like being forced to sit next to a ticking time bomb. It feels like it might explode at any minute. Desperation takes over and fleeing seems like the best option. It's not surprising that people who have these intense feelings of anxiety rely on avoidance to reduce their distress (that is, they take the "flight"—option) and believe that:

- I can't give that speech . . . everyone will see how nervous I am . . . I'm just going to fall apart up there . . . I just know I'll humiliate myself
- I don't know if I can travel that far to my cousin's wedding . . . I just don't feel like myself . . . what if I get sick . . . or what if we get lost on the way and then I get sick
- Since I'm sure these people will think I'm stupid—I won't go there
- My stomach is in a knot—I'd rather stay home
- I touched that sink . . . it's got germs all over it . . . I'd better wash my hands one more time just to make sure

In a nutshell, excessive anxiety steals pleasure from people's lives. At times, they are so overwhelmed with anxiety they can't function. Their fears and worry so dominate that other activities are significantly inhibited. Relief often comes from avoiding the anxiety by developing symptoms, rituals or protective lifestyle choices that provide some measure of feeling in control. And because their initial anxiety is reduced by performing these rituals, or by worrying and avoiding, these ineffective solutions become the primary means of escaping their discomfort. Once the way to avoid anxiety is established as a pattern of behavior, it's hard for that person to change. And it's also hard for you to watch them suffer.

Nevertheless, that's where you come in.

BECAUSE YOU CAN MAKE A DIFFERENCE

Whether you are dealing with a small problem or a big one, your interest and concern can make a difference. In essence no problem is too small. Helping someone manage a little problem can keep it from turning into a bigger one. Likewise, even problems that seem overwhelming and difficult can be alleviated when you know what to do and say. One of the things I most like about Claudia Strauss's book is that she gives you so many options to pick from. Because she has outlined so many possibilities, I'm confident that you will find something that will work for you.

Mental health specialists and physicians need your help. It's our job to diagnose and provide treatment for anxiety disorders. And fortunately, these problems are relatively easy to treat. But there are many reasons most people are reluctant to come for treatment, most of them couched in rationalizations such as "I can manage this myself," or "It's not that bad," or "I don't want pills" and "What good is talking about it?" You have probably heard all these excuses and more. But in *Talking to Anxiety*, you'll learn how to talk about getting help and how to make sure the help is actually helping.

Claudia Strauss is going to give you some down to earth advice on what to say and what to avoid. Whether you're the mother, son, teacher, friend, cousin, sister or coach, you'll discover that you'll feel less stuck when you uncover all the options outlined in this book. Your expressed concern coupled with the advice offered in *Talking to Anxiety* is all that is needed to make you more confident in providing the assistance you wish to offer.

You'll also learn something about what it feels like to be anxious all the time, or socially phobic or terrified of getting on an airplane or unnerved at the thought of another panic attack, or convinced that you must wash your hands now. And for each of these problems you learn what to say and what not to say. In addition, she provides you with an excellent resource guide so you'll know where to turn in order to get additional information and support.

Talking to Anxiety puts you on the road to real solutions for both yourself and the one you care enough about to help.

—Jeanne Albronda Heaton, Ph.D.
Counseling and Psychological Services,
Ohio University

Preface

Anxiety is a very difficult thing to live with and a very difficult thing to overcome. Over the years, I've known people who suffered from anxiety and people who struggled to understand and to help, and I've been in both positions myself. These experiences taught me a lot that I wish I'd known before. That's why I decided to tackle this book. Because when you are a friend or family member, or a neighbor or coworker, it's difficult to know what to say and how to say it, to know when to get involved and how deeply, to know what to do and what to avoid doing. I've tried to write the book I would like to have read, so you can hear from those who've been there—who know firsthand what helps and what does not, and who want to ease the road of those who follow them. Because there are two sets of sufferers: those who struggle with anxiety and those who care about them.

In this country, anxiety disorders affect approximately one in eight adults, which makes it very likely that most of us have someone in our lives we'd like to help. Yet most of us know even less about anxiety than we do about depression.

Professional help is out there—both medical and psychological—but there are so many hours in the day to get through, so many everyday tasks that need to be met, and the professionals can't be there all the time. It's the rest of us—the laypeople, the friends and neighbors and coworkers and family members—who live the day-to-day with the people we care about.

As much as we would like them to, not everyone will get the professional help that is available. Often, that's because they don't realize that what they are struggling with is something with a name, something that is treatable. But whether they get help or not, there are ways for us to provide support, encouragement, and validation. Anxiety can be scary and debilitating. It strips away self-respect and the ability to do things we take for granted. Anxiety isn't something fleeting that will dissipate once an upcoming event has passed. It is something that seems to take over and can't simply be shaken off.

You might wonder at that. You might think that everyone suffers from anxiety at some point and that it isn't such a big deal. But that's not the type of anxiety that is the subject of this book. It's the same word, but a very different animal. We do this a lot with medical terms, especially when it comes to emotion, mood, and mental health. We make words do double duty, and that is confusing. We take words for normal, everyday fluctuations in how we feel—such as depression and anxiety—and also use them for medical disorders that are as different from them as the common cold is from pneumonia or bronchitis or flu.

Yes, we do all suffer from common, garden-variety anxiety. We get nervous before a test or a speech, maybe get a stomachache before going to camp for the first time or starting a new job, feel our neck muscles tense up when we don't know the answer to a question, get dry in the mouth and see our hands tremble when we ask someone for a date. But we don't back off from *ever* doing those things again—and we don't come down with a fever or stop breathing at the very thought of doing them. Our nervousness, our anxiousness, may affect how we feel, but we don't let it stop our lives. We know where it's coming from—inexperience, lack of readiness, first-time jitters—and we know everyone gets these. We even know we've experienced this before, and we figure out a way to go on despite it.

An anxiety disorder is different. It's massive, pervasive, and it takes control. It's not a sign of weakness or evidence of a character flaw. It's an illness.

One in eight adults, and more than one in ten children, suffers from this kind of anxiety. I hope this book will help you see the difference. I hope this book will help you help them. Because you *can* make a difference.

FINDING YOUR WAY AROUND THIS BOOK

It might help you to know how this book is organized, because it doesn't necessarily need to be read in order.

This book addresses anxiety disorder in general: What it is, what it looks like, what it feels like, how you can help, what's best to say, what's best to do, what to expect, what to avoid doing and why, how an anxiety disorder is different from everyday, run-of-the-mill anxiousness, and how to walk in a sufferer's shoes.

For more specific types of tips, you can go straight to the appropriate chapters. For example, if you want to know what to say, go to part II; if you want an overview of anxiety, go to chapter 1; if you want some ideas about what to do, go to part III. There are also chapters on how anxiety affects kids and how to talk to them about it. One focuses on what to say when someone in their family is suffering from an anxiety disorder, and one focuses on how to support them when they are suffering from anxiety themselves.

The resource section suggests some key places where you can

get more information, where you can reach people who are living like you are living, and where you can connect with various forms of support. Chapter 19 suggests ways to take care of yourself and give to yourself while you are giving to others.

One of the most important chapters is the one about getting started (chapter 3), which focuses on the role you can play and your frame of mind. It will help you get on the right path and help make the support you give flow naturally from your life experience, your intuition, and your respect for the person who is suffering.

AN IMPORTANT NOTE

Because this book is a conversation with those of you who are trying to help, in the coming chapters when I say "we" I am referring to those of us who know someone struggling with an anxiety disorder. When I say "you" I am addressing you, the reader. And when I refer to those persons who are suffering from anxiety, I will use the third person. For some of you, the person you care about who is suffering from anxiety will be a man, and for others that person will be a woman, so I will sometimes use "he" and sometimes use "she" to achieve a balance.

I will also use the words "illness," "disorder," "disease," and "condition" interchangeably. These words tend to have different meanings for different people. What feels temporary to one person may feel permanent to another; what sounds treatable to you might sound intrinsic to someone else; what helps one person see the sufferer as a whole person might get in the way of someone else's ability to do that. In surveying a number of people over the years, I've found these four words resonate very differently. By using them interchangeably throughout this book, I hope to take the sting out of them, so we can concentrate on the person who is suffering and the positive things that are possible.

The focus of this book is on anxiety disorders in general and what you can do to be supportive when someone you know is struggling with one of them. However, from time to time the book zeroes in on specific forms of anxiety disorder where targeted suggestions could make a difference. These suggestions take into account some different approaches that need to be considered in terms of language, action, situations that can come up, and the context in which anxiety developed. Because there are so many variations to anxiety disorders, these brief targeted sections focus on a select few distinct conditions: phobias, obsessive-compulsive disorder, social anxiety, and post-traumatic stress disorder. If the person you care about suffers from one of these, those sections will supplement the general information in the chapter; if the person you care about suffers from one of the other forms of anxiety, the bulk of the book will help you provide the kind of support you want to give.

Finally, though this book is aimed at people who have persons in their lives who suffer from an anxiety disorder, many of the suggestions will be helpful in supporting those who are experiencing nonclinical anxiety as well.

Part I

Getting Started

"*First learn much, and then seek to understand it profoundly.*"

~ THE TALMUD

Chapter One

An Overview of Anxiety

ᘉ

*A*nxiety is a lonely place, and that isn't true just for the person who is suffering. It can be lonely for those of us who are struggling to help. It can feel as if we are standing by and watching as someone we care about is losing the things that make life worthwhile. We don't know what to do and we feel helpless.

It helps to know what we are dealing with, what exactly this thing called "anxiety" is. This chapter provides an overview of anxiety by answering commonly asked questions. After this explanatory chapter, the book will move on to hands-on help so that you can meet the various situations that arise—and, with growing confidence—reach for the words and actions that are supportive.

WHAT IS ANXIETY?

Anxiety is something that can get in the way of day-to-day functioning. It can prevent people from doing things they normally could do or prevent them from doing things that others would not think twice about doing. It can affect the general tenor of their day, every day, and what they feel to be their mood.

Anxiety causes people to be extremely worried, fearful, or horrified to the extent that it interferes with their ability to think, decide, or act, or interferes with their ability to be with certain people or go to specific places or perform particular actions. It is not what we ordinarily think of as simply being anxious or nervous; it differs in magnitude, in duration, and in quality. To the person who is suffering, it can feel as different in size as the Milky Way galaxy is compared to the planet Earth, as different in length as a century feels next to a minute, and as different in intensity as the whooping cough feels compared to clearing one's throat.

When people develop anxiety disorders, they need help to recover. Treatment can make a big difference to quality of life and there are a number of treatment approaches, which will be discussed in the next chapter.

WHO GETS ANXIETY?

Anyone can get it. It doesn't matter whether one is old or young, male or female, rich or poor, urban or rural. Nor does one's ethnic, religious, racial, or cultural background matter.

However, some people tend to develop anxiety disorders more than others, and some groups tend to be more susceptible to one form than others. Also, some people seem to be born with an anxiety disorder or develop it at a very young age.

HOW DEBILITATING IS IT?

That depends on the person, the form of anxiety, how severe it is, and whether it is likely to disrupt a person's regular routine. When anxiety is present all the time, it may be more disabling than when it is triggered only by certain circumstances. On the other hand, if someone is accustomed to planning for it on a daily basis, it may be disruptive but not cause as much distress. Both a person's reactions to his own anxiety and the reactions of those around him who are affected by it are also factors in how debilitating it is. The degree to which anxiety is disabling—interferes with normal routines, prevents someone from doing things, changes the way she did them, requires much more effort and time, or transforms relationships—can be assessed with some objective measures. However, how distressing it is and how long it seems to last tend to be more subjective and, for each person, that assessment can change over time.

Many people continue to function in their day-to-day lives, but not at the level they did before, often with considerable distress (that may be hidden from others) and often having to go to considerable lengths to manage. Others struggle to do the basics. Or there may be things they have cut from their lives for which they have offered reasonable explanations—such as not having time, trying to reduce stress, or having substituted something else—all of which are partially true, but not the whole truth. The symptoms may not all be visible to you; they may be things you sense.

In addition, sometimes it is the very lengths they have gone to in order to cope that turn out to be the most debilitating of all. It could be a system of behaviors she has put in place or a list of situations and people he is committed to avoiding. These can alienate other people, frustrate employers, take up inordinate amounts of time, and lead to restricted and isolated lives. Even when they see the negative results, they can't stop because they are afraid of losing control—even though what they created to make them feel more in control is now controlling them.

WHAT CAUSES ANXIETY?

Some forms of anxiety may run in families. A person is more likely to develop an anxiety disorder if someone else in the family has had one. This genetic predisposition doesn't mean that a person will develop an anxiety disorder, but one could be precipitated under certain environmental conditions.

Sometimes anxiety responses are learned. If a child grows up with parents who are very anxious and who don't have good ways of coping, that could influence her patterns of thinking and behavior. If children see that adults around them are confident about handling difficult situations, and have mastery over others, they will be much more likely to find that quality in themselves than if they are always exposed to adults who feel powerless and helpless. (This doesn't mean the parents are at fault in any way, only that what their children observe and experience could be a contributing factor. Parents influence children in all sorts of ways, and children vary in what they absorb, what they react to, and what they use.)

Other times anxiety begins as a normal response to an abnormal situation. If the abnormal situation continues, or keeps recurring, anxiety can become a conditioned response. For example, if children are abused, they will not only learn to be on guard but are likely to develop a startle response—they will be startled easily and to a greater degree—and will carry the anxiety that comes with it into adulthood. The more they are continually stressed in this way, the more vulnerable they will become because the chemical and nervous system responses that their bodies learn will become automatic. This abuse doesn't have to be direct; it could be directed at a brother or sister or at a parent; it could be observed secondhand from living in a violent neighborhood.

The stress of constant uncertainty or change can also create a pattern of anxiety responses. These responses could come from growing up in an alcoholic family or from frequent moves due to job changes or continual, repeated financial difficulties because the children who are vulnerable to anxiety never know if they can relax and settle down in school, in neighborhoods, with friends.

DOES ANYTHING MAKE IT MORE LIKELY FOR SOMEONE TO DEVELOP AN ANXIETY DISORDER?

Stress is associated with many modern ailments, and it is a factor in the development of anxiety, too. Ongoing stress can come from many parts of life—work, environmental, relationship, financial, legal, and medical issues. Severe forms of stress—such as traumatic events—can trigger anxiety, as can ongoing, long-term stress that doesn't seem to have any end in sight.

We know that stress and anxiety are related because people with ongoing stress and people with certain anxiety disorders have higher levels of chemicals such as cortisol and lower levels of chemicals such as serotonin in their systems—in their blood and in the fluid surrounding the brain. Cortisol is the hormone our adrenal glands produce in response to stress; serotonin is a neurotransmitter that helps to convey messages for the brain and is found in the gaps (or synapses) between nerves.

It's important to keep in mind, though, that stress is a part of life, that not all stress is bad, and that most people suffering from stress do not develop an anxiety disorder. For those who do, however, stress can be problematic.

WHAT ARE THE SYMPTOMS OF ANXIETY?

One could be a sudden resistance to doing things he used to do with no good reason for stopping, and getting angry (and seeming afraid) when urged to participate. Or it could be insisting on going the long way around when she usually takes the short way, without there seeming to be any rhyme or reason to it. These behaviors makes sense when you figure out the pattern. In both cases, the people suffering from anxiety are consistently avoiding something specific. People suffering from an anxiety disorder may freeze for no apparent reason, or become completely adamant (even obstinate) about a way of doing something, or have trouble dealing with something that has come as a surprise.

Other symptoms include an inability to slow down or relax, a sudden change in eating habits, a new level or frequency of irritability, or being nervous a lot of the time.

Some people may show different physical reactions. Often, they will start to breathe heavily, become short of breath, and start gasping. They may start to perspire, or shiver, or dart their eyes all around, or twist their hands together or clench them into fists. They may radiate tension or appear to shrink from the situation, or give the impression they are about to leave. They may tremble, get dizzy, feel chest pain from breathing problems or because their hearts are pounding.

If they start to hyperventilate or sound as if they are wheezing or barking, they could be having a panic attack. Panic attacks can be single, independent events, but they can also be an indication of an underlying anxiety disorder. In addition, they can be a sign of a specific form of anxiety called panic disorder. However, panic attacks have been seen with all forms of anxiety, and many people experience them. People who suffer from anxiety disorders can have panic attacks when faced with the *thought* of a threatening situation or when placed in an environment that reminds them of one, not just when actually placed in that situation. Panic attacks can also occur out of the blue—for no apparent reason at all.

The need to avoid threatening situations can lead people to gradually isolate themselves, as can the need to avoid exposing themselves and their reactions to other people.

WHAT ARE THE FORMS ANXIETY CAN TAKE?

Anxiety disorders fall into seven general categories: generalized anxiety disorder (GAD), acute stress disorder, post-traumatic stress disorder (PTSD), obsessive compulsive disorder (OCD), panic disorder, social anxiety disorder, and phobias.

The last one listed, phobias, is the category most people are familiar with. According to the Anxiety Disorders Association of America, it is also the most common, affecting over eleven million adults, or 8 percent of adult Americans between eighteen and fifty-four. (That number includes social anxiety disorder, which is sometimes grouped with phobias.)

The others cause a lot of suffering, too. Generalized anxiety disorder affects over four million adults; post-traumatic stress disorder affects over five million adults, as do social phobias; obsessive compulsive disorder affects over three million; and panic disorder affects over two million.

IS ANYONE MORE LIKELY TO GET A SPECIFIC ANXIETY DISORDER?

Yes. Generally, anxiety disorders tend to occur more often among women and younger people are more susceptible than older people. There are other distinctions as well. For example, studies have found that among Americans, people with a Caucasian background are more susceptible to OCD than people with an African, Asian, or Hispanic background.

And the gender distinction is not the same across all disorders. For example, OCD tends to be almost equally distributed between men and women; panic disorder, phobias, and generalized anxiety disorder tend to be diagnosed in women twice as often as in men. Falling somewhere in between, PTSD seems to be more common among women than among men. It is believed that domestic violence, sexual assaults, and other forms of sexual abuse and harassment are factors in the higher rate of PTSD in women; it's not clear why these gender differences exist for the other forms of anxiety. One possibility is that women may be more likely to be tested and to seek help.

How does generalized anxiety disorder (GAD) affect people?

People who suffer from GAD live with some level of anxiety all the time. The anxiety isn't about any particular threat or precipitated by any particular past experience, though there may be situations that can contribute to it or aggravate it.

Having a higher level of anxiety means that GAD sufferers may have trouble concentrating, could be easily distracted, may always be aware of what's going on around them, or might need to plan for things to avoid any surprises. They may have trouble making decisions, too, not because they don't know what they want but because they don't know how safe the situation will be or whether they will be able to control their reactions.

GAD is frightening for the people who struggle with it because, if it hasn't occurred to them that they might have an illness, they can't understand why they are so worried all the time or why their sleep is so interrupted.

What is panic disorder?

The hallmark of panic disorder is having panic attacks. These are unpredictable and seem to come out of nowhere. Though they don't last very long—typically about two minutes and sometimes as long as twenty minutes—they are very intense. They can overwhelm people with extremely strong feelings of apprehension, fear and terror.

Sufferers usually experience some physical symptoms. These can include shortness of breath, heart palpitations, chest pain, choking or smothering sensations, dizziness, feelings of unreality, tingling of their arms and legs, hot or cold flashes, sweating, faintness, trembling or shaking. Most people will have three or four of these feelings at any one time.

Because these attacks are very frightening, most people who have had one live in fear of having another. They fear losing control or think they are "going crazy" and will go out of their way to avoid anything they believe might trigger another attack.

Panic disorder can be the primary anxiety disorder someone suffers from or it can develop as part of another disorder.

When the panic attacks are due to the primary problem, some people will search for a pattern to the attacks. When they have one they might associate the place where it happened (say a mall), their purpose for being there, the time of day, the person they are with, or some other aspect simultaneous with the attack. They might not see this aspect as a coincidence; they may even see it as a determining factor. If they decide it was the mall, they might begin to avoid malls. Over time, they may amass quite a number of things to avoid, which will not only cut stimulation from their lives but may end up restricting them closer and closer to home. This can lead to their developing a phobia based on that avoidance such as panic disorder with social anxiety or panic disorder with agoraphobia.

This is all very sad because what people identify as triggers for their panic attacks might not be triggers at all. The panic attack may well have happened no matter where they were. It could just as easily have occurred at home—as panic attacks often do. However, once someone believes that there is a correlation, it can become true. And this is so both before and after they have ended up isolating themselves.

When the panic attacks are a secondary part of the diagnosis, they aren't so much a disorder as they are a way that someone responds to a different primary disorder. That makes the panic attacks more of a symptom than a cause. For example, someone might have a multiple diagnosis such as post-traumatic stress disorder with panic attacks. In that case, it is the PTSD that triggers the panic attacks, not the other way around.

WHAT DO PANIC ATTACKS LOOK LIKE?
Panic attacks take many forms and vary in intensity. Some people's throats close up and they have trouble talking and breathing. They may clutch their chests because of pain and pressure and think they are having a heart attack. The sounds coming from their mouths may resemble gasps, wheezing, a knocking sound, or high-pitched beats. They may get red in the face or gray. They may get light-headed. Their eyes may become fixed, or blank, or full of terror. They may be bathed in sweat. For some people, the heart beats so fast and so loud that it feels as if other people can actually see it beating. Sometimes, people get so frightened by the panic attack itself that their anxiety over the attack is greater than the anxiety that triggered it.

Panic attacks occur along a continuum: they can range from uncomfortable and relatively mild to severe enough for a trip to the emergency room. Usually they fall somewhere in between.

Panic attacks can even occur during sleep, and for many people these are the most frightening. They can also occur shortly after waking as a reaction to one's thoughts as one awakens.

WHAT IS POST-TRAUMATIC STRESS DISORDER?
This disorder, as its name indicates, is a result of trauma. The trauma can come from living through a natural disaster such as an earthquake or tornado, a threat to one's life or to someone one cares about, a rape or a hold-up at knifepoint, a home invasion, or a fire. It can come from a one-time event, from ongoing assaults, or from an everpresent threat of assault. These assaults can be physical or psychological—attacks on the mind or the body. What

they have in common is that they are threats one seems helpless to counter. The emotional abuse of constant, ongoing exposure to violence, whether in battle, as a victim of war, as the victim of domestic violence, or as the observer of this in one's home, can lead to the total undermining of trust, a persistent underlying layer of fear, and the constant prospect of flashbacks.

Living with these feelings is bad enough, but they can also lead to reactions, which though understandable, can damage their lives even further. For example, they can lead to panic attacks. These feelings can result in a need for total control of one's environment yet at the same time lead to a complete loss of control over oneself when any reminder makes them feel threatened. Many people suffer reactions to traumas like this for a period of weeks or months and gradually regain functioning and trust and the ability to live their lives. But for some people the flashbacks never stop, the fear never goes away, and the avoidance of situations with any similarity to the environment they were in when it happened is still a focus of their lives. When this persists, and the other anxiety symptoms persist as well, then the person may have developed PTSD.

When a person suffers from PTSD, the places to avoid could include hospitals and courtrooms as well as battlefields, parking lots, particular street corners, or anyplace a particular person or type of person might be likely to appear. Seeing, hearing, smelling, touching, interacting in any way with the places and people associated with the trauma is not a reasoned decision but a visceral one—a deep revulsion, horrible dread, and excruciating pain. But these can lead to the reasoned decision not to subject oneself to these experiences and to limit even any anticipation of them, because they can put someone right back in the original traumatic situation and make them feel as if it were happening again.

What are some things to know about
traumatic memories?

Some people have vivid nightmares that recur. In addition, they might have flashbacks during the day that make them feel they are reliving the traumatic experience. Sometimes these will be accompanied by panic attacks, sometimes by intense physical pain, sometimes by intense shaking or sobbing, sometimes by complete withdrawal. This withdrawal can be so complete that a person can lose blocks of time. He could just sit facing a wall and come to himself a couple of hours later thinking only a few minutes had passed. Flashbacks can also be accompanied by intense fear, rage, anger, images from a past event, and overreaction to events.

A true flashback experience, though rare, is terrifying. It can take over so completely that the present completely disappears and only the memory seems real. Vivid dreams can be terrifying too, because when the feelings are intense and seem to duplicate the original experience, they will feel almost like a flashback.

One of the hardest things about a flashback it that once it is switched on there is no easy way to switch it off. It doesn't just stop; the person can be engulfed by it and the flashback can take on a life of its own.

Whether the person with PTSD gets flashbacks or not, she tends to be under constant stress from memories and reminders, and from the need to continually revamp whatever strategies she is using to cope. Unless she is fighting for someone else's life (such as her child's), or is trapped in a domestic violence situation she cannot escape, she will avoid situations that are tormenting and she will focus on rebuilding her life and on giving herself space to heal. Forcing her into these situations can cause further trauma. (More on this in chapter 2.)

People suffering from PTSD can react in an extreme way to a similar event—even of very small threat or intensity—as if it were a repeat of the original trauma because, to the person dealing with PTSD, it can feel as if it is happening again in real time, right now. And it doesn't have to be an event. All kinds of associations can trigger the panic attacks, including just thinking about being exposed to the environment in which the original trauma occurred.

For most people, the challenge is controlling the onslaught of memories. The trauma doesn't go away. It is always there. But it is not always there in the same way. Picture a painting. It has a foreground, a midground, and a background. Imagine the thoughts in your mind shifting from one position to another. When they are not in the foreground, it doesn't mean they aren't there. We are conscious of them, yet we manage to put more focus elsewhere. The closer to the foreground they are and the more we have to deal with them, the harder it is to carry out the tasks before us. For people suffering from PTSD, it is an ongoing daily struggle to keep the memories out of the foreground and to try to tune out the voices, sounds, smells, feelings and images that keep crowding in. People who suffer from PTSD are often operating on two planes at once. We can't see it, but living this way requires an extraordinary amount of strength and self-discipline, not to mention a keen sense of responsibility to the people in their lives.

Whatever the cause, the wound is never only physical. It is the psychological pain, the emotional abuse, that takes the longest to heal.

HOW WOULD I RECOGNIZE OBSESSIVE COMPULSIVE DISORDER?

OCD is very difficult to spot because people try very hard to hide it.

OCD stands for obsessive compulsive disorder. Obsessions are thoughts—things the sufferer is worried about, such as hygiene, safety, fear of harming someone, or that someone might harm his child—that he will constantly go over and over in his head. Compulsions are actions—the things she will do proactively to reduce her anxiety over the obsession. These actions may include things we associate with OCD, such as a need to keep everything just so or an intense effort to maintain personal cleanliness, but these examples are not representative of everyone who is struggling with OCD.

People suffering from OCD often have rituals they need to follow—such as detailed routines—before they can leave the house or settle down to work. A ritual will have a number of steps that have to be followed rigorously and in order. If a step is missed or interrupted, many people have to start over again. This can make something that would usually involve half an hour of preparation take up to two or three hours.

Sufferers will also repeat their ritual when they are not sure they have completed it properly. The rest of us might go back inside the house a couple of times to double- and-triple-check that we've turned something off or put something away or locked the door properly. Someone with OCD might need to recheck a dozen times.

People with OCD, as with other anxiety disorders, tend to isolate themselves to avoid embarrassment. If someone stops making any morning appointments, or is constantly very late for them or never shows up at all, it could be because the rituals just took too long. The same is true for social engagements. If time after time they don't make it when they said they would and they always have some sort of excuse, it could also be because the rituals took over.

Some people struggling with OCD also have a tendency to hoard things, to the extent that if you do have the opportunity to visit them at home, you'll find all kinds of barriers to walking around because all the floor space has been given over to things saved and kept. Hoarding can be particularly difficult to treat.

Also, if you think someone is developing eccentricities he didn't have before, this could be a sign of OCD.

WHAT SHOULD I KNOW ABOUT PHOBIA?

Phobias include such things as social anxiety disorder and many different specific (or simple) phobias, including agoraphobia and claustrophobia. We often tend to think of people's phobias as quirks of personality that are on the fringes of their lives. Sometimes that is true but, for other people, phobias can be at the center of their lives, limiting recreational choices, career choices, whom they can visit, where they can go, how they can get there, and even where they live. The degree to which a phobia can derail a life or limit the way it is lived depends on the type of phobia, its severity, a person's dreams and aspirations, and the expectations of the people around him.

There are numerous specific phobias to a vast variety of places, situations, diseases, animals, objects, and activities. These can range from heights to depths, from open spaces to closed spaces, from snakes to bees, from blood to needles, from the dentist's chair to sitting anywhere, from hospitals to germs, from crossing bridges to crossing streets, from thunder to noise in general, from flying to trains, from water to fire, from crowds to being alone, from numbers to colors, from darkness to light.

People with a specific phobia generally know exactly what it is they are afraid of and they avoid both being near it as well as thinking about being near it. They are very uncomfortable about their fear because they know it is unreasonable and beyond their control. They not only fear the thing itself, but they fear their response to it—because they know that being exposed to it or even anticipating being exposed to it will trigger an anxiety response.

Maybe they'll have a panic attack. Maybe they'll freeze and not even be able to walk away from the situation. Maybe they will react in a way that appears very unreasonable to us and out of proportion to what is happening. Maybe they'll get dizzy and faint.

What you will see is an extreme and frequently-occurring reaction. For example, rather than taking shelter during a thunderstorm, he might hide in a closet or under a bed. Rather than saying she is allergic to some cats and asking that the cat be kept in a different room during her visit, she might lock herself in a bathroom and cower in the bathtub. And he might insist that his doctor do monthly blood tests indefinitely even though no antibodies for any sexually transmitted disease have ever been found, he has continued to use protection, and has been consistently monogamous.

The anxiety response in itself is scary and painful; the humiliation of other people witnessing the terror is scary and painful, too. So people with a specific phobia, depending on what it is, how likely they are to encounter its cause, and how severe it is, will arrange their lives around never having to run into it at all. In some cases, you may never know of someone's phobia unless a situation suddenly arises that couldn't be planned for and you witness it.

EXAMPLES OF SPECIFIC PHOBIAS
WITH THEIR SCIENTIFIC AND COMMON NAMES

Agoraphobia—fear of open spaces or crowded, public spaces

Acrophobia—fear of heights

Ailurophobia—fear of cats

Arachnophobia—fear of spiders

Aviophobia—fear of flying

Brontophobia—fear of thunder and lightning

Ceraunophobia—fear of thunder

Claustrophobia—fear of closed spaces

Entomophobia—fear of insects

Hemophobia—fear of blood

Herpetophobia—fear of reptiles

Hydrophobia—fear of water

Paraskavedekatriaphobia—fear of Friday the 13th

Photophobia—fear of light

Pyrophobia—fear of fire

Thanatophobia—fear of death

Triskaidekaphobia—fear of the number thirteen

Xenophobia—fear of strangers (or foreigners)

Zoophobia—fear of animals

How is social anxiety disorder different from shyness?

Social anxiety disorder may look like shyness, but it is on another level entirely. People who are shy may feel some discomfort around strangers or not want to be in situations where there are large groups of people. People with social anxiety disorder will feel a tremendous amount of distress, sometimes even in familiar situations with family members. What they feel is much more pervasive, and it can prevent them from participating in many everyday functions, not just ones that come up now and then. They are not just shy—they are afraid. Afraid they may do something embarrassing, such as turn red, faint, run away, freeze, or just stand there speechless. Afraid they won't know anyone, or that if someone new appears that they may start shaking and sweating profusely. And they fear this will be obvious to everyone.

Social anxiety disorder doesn't just affect social occasions, it affects work, too. Many of us get nervous about being asked to present something at a meeting. People with social anxiety disorder are afraid that they will be asked to attend. Afraid someone might ask their opinion on something. Afraid that everyone will turn to look at them.

How common is agoraphobia?

Agoraphobia is the most common phobia. Agoraphobia tends to be one of the most isolating phobias because it can prevent someone from leaving the house for any reason. In its more severe forms, the person suffering from it might be unable to go into the backyard, go out to pick up the mail, open the front door to pick up the newspaper on the mat, or even have trouble looking out the window.

Agoraphobia is easy to treat, except for one major roadblock—the challenge of getting the person to the treatment. She may want to get help but be unable to go. When the treatment can come to the person, it may be painstaking and slow, but it is usually successful. However, though not as reinforcing as face-to-face therapy, Internet support groups can be of help and might be worth a try.

DOES ANXIETY ALWAYS LOOK LIKE ANXIETY?

No. Anxiety might come out in more than one way. An indication that people might be suffering from anxiety is the presence of aches and pains that won't go away, don't respond to medical treatment, and for which doctors can't find an immediate physical cause. These might include such things as headaches, stomachaches, chest pain, neck pain, back pain, achy eyes, or jaw pain. This is particularly true of children.

If the symptoms are severe and disabling—such as weakness, fainting, persistent nausea, urinary problems, extraordinary and debilitating fatigue, or even temporary paralysis or blindness—and doctors can't find any physical causes, the person may be suffering from a related disorder in which anxiety can play a part. About 2 percent of Americans suffer from one of these related disorders called somatoform disorders. Because anxiety plays a part in somatoform disorders, treating anxiety will help people recover, and the same kind of support from the people around them can make a significant difference, too. This means that being aware of the existence of somatoform disorders, what they look like, and how they affect people, can help you to make that difference.

This is particularly important because people suffering from somatoform disorders will be focused on their physical symptoms. Many might not feel tense or worried; either way they will see the physical symptoms as isolated from other things going on in their lives. It may not occur to them that anxiety could be involved.

The symptoms can be scary, and people react to them in various ways. They can lead someone to think he has a serious or life-threatening disease. On the other hand, depending on the symptoms, someone else might not be concerned at all. And a third person might think his body is defective and live his life around that.

If a person is experiencing severe symptoms with no apparent cause—which is to say that doctors can't find any physical causes that fit with the severity of the symptoms—it is also possible that they are missing the problem or don't have the means to diagnose it. Autoimmune diseases, for example, are very difficult to diagnose. Unfortunately, if the symptoms are caused by a somatoform disorder, the person you care about may get a double whammy of anxiety—he might interpret these physical symptoms as meaning he has a serious disease. Now he has the anxiety that contributed to these symptoms in the first place as well as the anxiety he feels from having these symptoms go unexplained or untreated. That can be challenging for everyone involved.

Doctors don't start out with a diagnosis of a somatoform disorder. They will search for the typical causes of specific aches and pains. If these are ruled out, a chemical imbalance may be suspected, and the possibility of a disorder such as anxiety or depression might be considered. Chemical imbalances in the brain are physical causes, too, but there are no tests available to measure them directly. For now, chemical imbalance is generally diagnosed through the presence of symptoms combined with the ruling out of other ailments that *can* be confirmed through laboratory tests. There is still a lot of art to the practice of medicine.

If doctors can't uncover anything else to account for symptoms and suspect that an anxiety disorder might have a role in what is happening, they will suggest a renewed focus on the mind/body connection to give the mind a chance to take a more conscious role in healing.

Sometimes that can mean trying treatment approaches for anxiety to see if they work. In effect, the treatment approach is used as a diagnostic tool. If the symptoms are lessened, that will suggest that anxiety plays a role. If there is no change, that will suggest professionals look elsewhere.

Sometimes people with somatoform disorders feel the diagnosis can't be right, that it's the physical symptom that should count, that the doctor is saying it's all in their heads. It helps to remember that our minds and bodies are inseparably connected, that each affects the other, that there is a constant ongoing feedback loop in place. Just as this is true for mild aches and pains, it can be true for more severe ones. Our bodies react to stress by tensing up muscles, breathing more shallowly, and pumping blood faster, and we can consciously affect that by breathing deeply, slowing down our thoughts, and stretching our muscles. With treatment, people can learn to affect the unconscious processes, too.

If I suspect someone is suffering from an anxiety disorder, what should I do?

It is not your job to be a diagnostician. You don't have the knowledge, the training, the experience, or the skills. However, if you see several symptoms of anxiety, they seem to be intense, they are causing the person you care about a lot of distress, and they are present over a period of time, say two weeks, then the person you care about may be suffering from an anxiety disorder.

You can suggest he see a doctor for a work-up. Maybe he is

suffering from something else that produces similar symptoms. Maybe she has a deficiency in a vitamin or mineral or is not producing enough of a particular enzyme or hormone. Maybe the levels of an enzyme or hormone are too high. Maybe he is suffering side effects from a medication he is taking. Maybe it is something that should get immediate attention, such as a tumor. There are many different kinds of illnesses that could produce symptoms similar to those of an anxiety disorder. A doctor may identify something else that can be treated.

WHAT HAPPENS IF OTHER AILMENTS ARE RULED OUT?

The doctor may refer him to someone else who could assess whether he is suffering from an anxiety disorder and, if so, which one. That person could be a psychiatrist, a psychologist, a therapist, or a counselor. Once they have a diagnosis to work with, the person you care about and the specialist can work together to decide on a course of treatment, what kind of professional would be best, and if more than one approach were to be used, how they would be coordinated. (Note that insurance companies are more likely to recognize a diagnosis from a medical doctor or licensed psychologist and may have restrictions on what professionals they will cover for treatment.)

ARE ANY OTHER DISORDERS OR DISEASES ASSOCIATED WITH ANXIETY?

Many people who suffer from anxiety also suffer from depression. This means that you might see a mixture of symptoms, which could make it difficult to tell what is going on. It also means that there may be two different disease processes that should be addressed. It would not be enough to treat only one of them.

Common symptoms of depression include: changes in sleeping patterns, excessive fatigue, changes in eating patterns, lack of interest in things that used to give pleasure, inability to concentrate, persistent feelings of hopelessness, deep feelings of worthlessness, continual restlessness or irritability, and thoughts of death or suicide. You may also see physical manifestations such as weight loss, weight gain, or constant headaches or colds. If you see at least five of these symptoms consistently over a period of two weeks, it is possible that the person you care about is suffering from depression.

There are other conditions that can coexist with an anxiety disorder. For example, diseases that affect the workings of the brain can often be accompanied by anxiety. People suffering from Alzheimer's disease will often develop anxiety, as will people with traumatic brain injury that could come from an accident or a fall, or people who have suffered a stroke. If the part of the brain called the prefrontal cortex is damaged in some way, people can end up having fears that are exaggerated or seem to come out of nowhere—with no cause or source anyone can identify. (In addition, people who care for loved ones who are suffering from dementia are at risk for anxiety themselves.)

Moreover, people often suffer from more than one anxiety disorder at a time, or from other disorders as well as anxiety disorders. OCD and panic disorder often occur concurrently, as do agoraphobia and panic disorder. It is not uncommon to see OCD co-occur with attention deficit disorder (ADD or ADHD) or with pervasive developmental disorder (PDD). PDD is a relatively new term; sometimes the phrase "autism spectrum disorders" is used instead. In PDD, a person's symptoms are similar to autism but not as severe. Other combinations of anxiety disorders, or of anxiety disorders with another condition, can coexist as well. (See the discussion of somatoform disorders earlier in this section.)

PEOPLE WHO SUFFER FROM DEPRESSION ARE AT RISK FOR SUICIDE. IS THIS TRUE FOR PEOPLE WHO SUFFER FROM ANXIETY?

Generally, no. But if they are also struggling with clinical depression, they might be. If they talk about death or suicide, start giving possessions away, have a plan for how to do it, and have the means, then you should contact an emergency hotline or your local hospital right away.

On the other hand, people suffering from post traumatic stress disorder may be at higher risk for suicide attempts, and accidents. Men who have suffered PTSD because of war or violent crimes are at particular risk of becoming violent themselves. Women tend to be at higher risk for suicide and being re-victimized.

While some people withdraw, the combination of pain and fear can also cause people to lash out in different ways. Sometimes their feelings are just so hard to contain and at other times their keenest wish is to escape them. This can lead to accidents, to violence, and other forms of mental and physical distress. It's important to keep in mind, though, that if someone doesn't have a history of violence, the chances of that are greatly reduced. The only truly reliable predictor of violence is violence.

WHY DOES ANXIETY MAKE PEOPLE VULNERABLE TO SUBSTANCE ABUSE?

People who are struggling with social anxiety disorder, in particular, tend to self-medicate in order to face and get through social situations. For them, it is the anxiety that is the underlying cause of drinking, addictive behavior, and the use of street drugs. Treating the substance abuse alone will not get at the root of the problem.

Other forms of anxiety can also lead to substance abuse. When people are feeling particularly vulnerable, such as PTSD sufferers, or when they are feeling out of control, such as OCD sufferers, they will turn to something that they think can either bolster them, calm them down, or make them feel they are taking some sort of constructive action. (To get an idea of the scope, up to 20 percent of people with an alcohol problem are suffering from an anxiety disorder.)

People suffering from anxiety need to be careful about drugs because often they will increase the anxiety symptoms instead of decreasing them. This is especially true of stimulants, whether legal or illegal, and includes such drugs as caffeine, nicotine, cocaine, and amphetamines.

Also, it is not just taking the drug in itself that can increase anxiety symptoms. The process of withdrawing from drugs can produce anxiety reactions and increase symptoms someone already has. This makes it even more difficult to quit taking those drugs. In this case, anxiety is *not* the underlying problem, but the sufferer may think it is. Instead, it is the body's nervous system trying to readjust after having been sedated for a period of time. This can happen after a weekend of binge drinking, or it can happen when a person tries to cut down on these kinds of drugs: alcohol, barbiturates, benzodiazepines, cannabinoids, or opiates. Barbiturates include Amytal, Butisol, and "downers"; benzodiazepines include Valium, Ativan, Xanax, and Halcion; cannabinoids include hemp and marijuana; opiates include heroin, morphine, and codeine.

What this means is that when people add drugs to anxiety, both the substance abuse and the anxiety can look different. And both the sufferer and the people in his life—friends, family, coworkers, coaches, and medical professionals—can be confused by that.

WHY DOES ANXIETY MAKE PEOPLE VULNERABLE TO SELF-ABUSE?

This is a form of self-medicating, too. Some people who are suffering inflict physical harm on themselves in the effort to release some of the pain that comes with anxiety. Doing this gives them the sense—unfortunately only temporarily—that there is a small way in which they can exert control over what they feel.

Self-abuse can take the form of cutting the skin or legs until they bleed, or the form of burning the skin with cigarettes. Though apparently much less common than substance abuse, the fact is that people who do it are careful to hide it. Once thought to be mostly a thing that teens and college students do, it is now recognized that adults quietly turn to these forms of release, too. It is important to realize that, unlike other dramatic behaviors young people might engage in, this is not an attempt to get attention. If it were, those doing it would not work so hard to hide it.

DOES ANXIETY AFFECT QUALITY OF LIFE IN ANY OTHER WAYS?

Yes. It can affect memory and libido. And it can affect the immune system, which makes sufferers more susceptible to infectious diseases and can lower their ability to bounce back. That can slow or even impede recovery from heart attacks, strokes, surgical procedures, and influenza.

Anxiety also affects a person's health in other ways. It puts people at risk for developing ulcers, high blood pressure, irregular heart rhythms, asthma, irritable bowel syndrome, back pain, headaches, strokes, and heart attacks.

All of this makes it important to consider treatment, which is the subject of the next chapter.

"So many times I have been told that I must not offer fishes to men but rods so that they can fish for themselves. Ah! My God! So often they do not have the strength to hold the rods. Giving them fish I help them to recover the strength necessary for the fishing of tomorrow."

ॐ MOTHER TERESA

Chapter Two

Help Is Available

꒐

THINGS TO KNOW ABOUT TREATMENT

*P*eople who suffer from an anxiety disorder have a lot of physical and emotional pain. They shiver and they sweat. They feel chest pain and pain in their gut. Their skin crawls and their jaws lock. They get headaches and allergies. Their bowels revolt and either refuse to pass anything or never stop running. They feel nervous, afraid, insecure. They can't face people or issues or the outside world. They don't know how to escape their inside world. The same thoughts go round and round in their heads and they can't turn them off or shut them out. When they do succeed, it takes all their energy and nothing else can come in. Either way, they are paralyzed. This means that they struggle to accomplish the basics of living: eating, breathing, talking, walking, making decisions, and getting things done.

As a result, anxiety disorders will affect relationships, tax marriages and family life, interfere with the ability to perform a job, derail careers, and attack a person's very sense of self.

The sooner the disorder is addressed, the more likely that it will come under control or even go away. The longer one waits, the more likely it will become entrenched, get worse, be something that will wax and wane for years to come.

This chapter provides some background information on the

different treatment options available, explains why getting help is important, and explores why a person suffering from anxiety might refuse professional help. Chapter 8, Words That Help, will discuss ways to encourage someone to seek help. The rest of the book will focus on what you, as a layperson, can do or say to be supportive.

TREATMENT APPROACHES

There are a number of ways to treat anxiety, including both medical/pharmacological and counseling/therapeutic approaches. The choice of treatment depends on the person and the type of anxiety disorder. Often, combining the two approaches works best because medications can balance out the chemistry in the body and take the edge off what a person is feeling. This makes it possible for him to benefit from counseling.

A number of other treatment techniques are often included, ranging from biofeedback, relaxation techniques, and visualization to acupuncture, yoga, dietary management, and eye movement therapy.

It is believed that over time the brain establishes a pathway—controlled by the production and then routing of chemicals—that causes an anxiety response to become automatic. So an objective of treatment is to retrain the sufferer's brain—changing the amount of chemicals produced and establishing different pathways—to respond without anxiety.

The use of medications to control the level of agitation, the teaching of coping strategies such as relaxation techniques to control intensity and duration, and the use of diet to suppress anxiety all make it possible for this kind of retraining to take place. Even simple things, such as reducing the intake of caffeine, can make a difference, particularly in GAD, because caffeine can raise the level of anxiety.

MEDICATION

More and more, antidepressants are being used to treat anxiety—partly because if depression is present, both are being addressed at the same time—and partly because unlike many antianxiety medications, antidepressants do not have a sedative effect and are less likely to be addicting.

Another reason antidepressants have become favored is that doctors have observed a similar correlation between reduced levels of serotonin and the presence of symptoms both in people suffering from anxiety and in people suffering from depression. Then, when serotonin levels are restored to normal levels, they have seen that the symptoms of both anxiety and depression tend to lessen significantly or even disappear. So finding ways to increase serotonin makes sense.

However, medication alone is often not enough. Though sometimes the medication itself is the primary mode of treatment, in many cases it is part of an overall strategy to provide comprehensive treatment. The medication delivers some temporary relief and makes it possible for counseling approaches to provide treatment that will lead to more effective, long-term solutions.

COUNSELING APPROACHES

Professionals have a lot of experience applying cognitive/behavioral therapies to both anxiety and mood disorders and these approaches have been found to work well. What helps to make them work are the empathy of the therapist, the motivation of the sufferer, and a good fit (including good chemistry) between the two. Sometimes it can take a while to find a good fit, so the person suffering from anxiety shouldn't give up on finding the right person.

For phobias, the specific behavioral approach called desensitization is very effective. The phobia is broken down into all its components, and then the sufferer gradually gets accustomed to one component after another—first from a distance for a very short period of time and in a "rehearsed" atmosphere. Gradually the person will get closer and closer to each component for longer periods. Then the components will be combined. The rehearsal could be physically in a staged area made to look like the real thing, or it could even be in one's imagination at first. Sometimes distance, time and staging could be worked on simultaneously; at other times they could be worked on separately.

Post-traumatic stress disorder is sometimes approached in this way, but it depends very much on the individual, the source of the trauma, the way that person thinks and processes information, whether the trauma was a single event or an ongoing or recurrent situation, whether it is indeed over, and how long it has been since it was definitively over. For many people with PTSD, the techniques of desensitization are not appropriate and they can intensify, prolong, and deepen the post-traumatic response. To avoid this, the professional will respect the person's own perceived readiness for this approach and her receptivity to attempting it.

Sometimes a cousin of desensitization is the treatment of choice for PTSD. There are a variety of talk therapy approaches that might ask people to relive the traumatic event and develop control over it as they relive it in their minds. The more a person is oriented to self-analysis and coming up with insights about herself, the more she can talk about the event with a little distance and perspective rather than sinking into it, and the more she can perceive what's realistic and what's not, the more suitable this therapy would be. When this is appropriate, the sufferer has the opportunity to express anger and rage, and to see the event from the outside. This enables her to regain things she has lost, and to feel a sense of power and control.

Panic disorder is particularly responsive to cognitive and behavioral therapies. These approaches teach the person experiencing panic attacks to recognize what is happening and understand it for what it is, and give the person ways to cope with a panic attack when one occurs and a sense of how long it is likely to last. Understanding the physiological reactions he is experiencing during an attack is a critical part of the therapy.

The sense of understanding and control this gives someone who has been suffering from panic attacks can actually decrease the intensity of future attacks. This is because a big part of panic attacks is the anxiety that hits about the attack itself. Now, it is possible that this secondary anxiety—often a fear that one is having a heart attack and is about to die—won't be triggered.

Treatment for obsessive compulsive disorder is very specialized, and many local areas around the country may not have someone with the training and experience to offer effective treatment. Treatment involves an intensive, short-term behavioral program tailored to the individual and often includes medication so that the person can relax his thinking enough to benefit from the therapy.

INVOLVING FRIENDS AND FAMILY

Sometimes it helps for friends and family members to get involved in the treatment process. People suffering from an anxiety disorder don't always know what initially caused their phobia or don't remember what has led to post-traumatic stress reactions. Sometimes this is because they have repressed what has happened to them; sometimes it is because they don't associate what is happening now with what happened then; sometimes it is because of something that occurred when they were so young that they have no memory of it. If friends or family remember an event that could be associated with it, therapy can help to put it in perspective and diminish its effect in the future.

However, people undergoing treatment often prefer to keep therapy one-on-one and the details of what they are going through completely private. So the professional will only agree to your involvement in the treatment process if that is something the person you care about wants. Unless the person is at risk of hurting himself or someone else, or a judge rules otherwise, the professional cannot reveal anything about the person he is helping. Only the person in therapy can sign a release form that allows the therapist to talk about what is happening.

IF YOU SUSPECT THERE ARE THINGS THE PROFESSIONAL DOESN'T KNOW

Sometimes you might have information that can be helpful to the therapist. You might be seeing behaviors that the therapist is unlikely to see and that the person you care about is unlikely to mention. Someone suffering from anxiety might not report something because it doesn't occur to him or because he doesn't realize there has been a change. It can be difficult to stand outside oneself and notice such things. Someone with OCD, particularly, may not realize how severe the OCD has become, or it could be that she avoids mentioning what is happening because she doesn't want to appear to be getting worse.

You want the therapist to have information that will be useful for treatment, but you also want the person you care about to be comfortable about your providing information. Though you don't need a consent form to provide information (the therapist only has to listen), it's a good idea to talk to the person suffering from anxiety about how he feels about your passing on observations that could end up helping him. Most of the time you will probably want to honor his feelings. Depending on your relationship, how much of a difference you think the information could make, and the degree to which this might increase his anxiety, you might go ahead anyway, but be sure not to do this behind his back. Tell him you are doing it because of your concern. You might also consider having him first discuss the pros and cons of your sharing information with his therapist as part of his deciding how he feels about it. If he tells her that a friend is noticing some things, he might give some examples and the information will have been transmitted anyway.

When would you go ahead without permission? If you feel the person you care about is in danger or is lying to the therapist. In addition, you must be willing to have the therapist acknowledge that the information came from you so she can make effective use of it.

MAKING TREATMENT WORK

When people have a good fit with the professionals they work with and when they follow through on the treatment plan they are given, many can recover completely. Others can be free of symptoms for years. Still others will learn coping strategies and compensating techniques that allow them to resume their lives.

Keep in mind that there are no five-minute cures. People who begin taking medications for anxiety may be unfamiliar with the way they work and may stop taking them abruptly before they've really done their job. They may stop taking them because they don't think they are working or because they seem to have already made a difference. Stopping medication too soon can set a person back—it can make the anxiety come back and it can intensify the symptoms.

First, it is important to give the medication time to work. Some medications can be taken as needed; some need to be taken consistently for a period of time. The doctor should make clear which kind of medication she is prescribing and, if it is to be taken over a period of time, how long that time should be before someone can tell if it is making a difference. This is because some medications take time to build up in the body and start kicking in. Others take time to fully accomplish what they've set out to do. For example, we know that we may feel better within a couple of days of starting an antibiotic, but we know we have to take it for the complete number of days and dosages to really knock out whatever has infected us.

The same is true for anxiety medication. Some people experience side effects on anxiety medications for a couple of weeks before they feel any of the benefits, and this can make them give up on the treatment. It's okay to ask the doctor whether there will be side effects and how long they will last; they often tend be much less of an issue or even go away entirely once the benefits of the medication start to kick in.

Understanding what side effects to expect is important. It makes it easier to live with the mild, ordinary ones and not have something to worry about. And it can help a person recognize a side effect that is unusual or particularly intense so that the doctor can be alerted right away. A small percentage of people can have extreme reactions to certain medications. These are not side effects but an inability to tolerate specific medications similar to an allergy or intolerance to other things in one's environment. Someday, doctors will be able to screen people via genetic markers; in the meantime, the people who experience these rare extreme reactions should switch medications. If someone has *new* symptoms *after* starting a medication, and they include such things as extreme distress, panic attacks, loss of appetite, withdrawal, insomnia, and agitation to the degree that she is functioning less rather than more, the doctor should know right away so he can take action. The person you care about shouldn't stop the medication on her own because some medications need to be tapered off gradually.

IF TREATMENT ISN'T WORKING

It's important that the person suffering from anxiety ask the doctor or therapist about what kind of progress should be expected and when it should be expected, and for him to communicate to the doctor what kind of changes he is seeing (or not seeing). Medication can be added or changed. Dosages can be adjusted. Therapy can be added or changed or adjusted, too.

If treatment isn't working, professionals may consult someone else or decide to refer the person you care about to someone else. And if they haven't incorporated complementary or holistic medicine approaches, they may decide to do so now.

IF SOMEONE DOESN'T WANT TREATMENT

People resist getting treatment for a number of reasons. Unless they are a threat to themselves or to others, you can't force them to get help. However, it is a good idea to encourage them to do so.

Why don't they want treatment? It's not so much that they don't want to recover, but they dread the process of admitting the problem, working with a stranger, maybe even leaving the house. They feel this must be a weakness, somehow their fault, something they should be able to handle themselves. They may feel ashamed that they can't handle it and fear the embarrassment of anyone else knowing about it. Cost is a factor, too, as is familiarity. As much as they hate what the anxiety is doing to them, it is also a familiar place, and being forced to do something they are afraid to do—leave this place and admit what is happening—is part of their terror, part of their anxiety. This is particularly difficult if they are suffering from social anxiety disorder or agoraphobia or obsessive compulsive disorder.

Some people don't believe they have a mental illness; they see eccentricity. They see it as something one lives with just as one lives with a limp or some other minor debilitating ailment. Or they resist any sort of label because they think it would mean they are "crazy." They don't recognize that this is a disorder of the brain—something physical—not a disease of the mind or a stain on their character.

Some people recognize that their symptoms could be defined as an illness, but they don't believe there is a way out. If they have attempted treatment before and it was ineffective, they may be unwilling to try again. They may feel the diagnosis and the treatment don't apply to them.

Older adults, in particular, tend to be very leery of medical treatment for anxiety. This is because in the fifties and sixties, when they were young adults and raising families, anxiety was seen as a weakness, as something that housewives fell victim to, and the treatment for it led to chemical addiction. We know now that anxiety affects men, women, and children. That it is not a weakness but a treatable illness. Medications are much safer today, and doctors monitor people closely for reactions, appropriate dosages, and dependency. So many older adults need to see evidence of these changes before they can seek help.

THE RISKS OF NOT GETTING TREATMENT

When they don't get treatment, people run the risk of not getting better, of getting worse, of suffering many other kinds of losses in the realm of home, work, and friendships. The risk of developing other illnesses or compounding other health problems they already have. The risk of developing more and more compensating strategies that are counterproductive, perversely increasing their anxiety and further isolating them from regular life. (For example, when someone has a phobia, he is likely to avoid any kind of exposure to the thing he dreads. The lack of exposure will reduce his anxiety temporarily, but it will reinforce the phobia. This, in turn, can intensify his feelings of anxiety over time.)

Let them know the risks of not getting treatment. Let them know that treatment is available and that it works. Let them know how much you would respect their taking charge of the situation by consulting a professional.

Offer to help make an appointment. Offer to go along. It is very difficult to overcome an anxiety disorder on one's own.

"*What we love is . . . your radiance.
It is that which you know not in yourself.*"

∽ RALPH WALDO EMERSON

Chapter Three

What To Do First

༄

BEFORE YOU GET STARTED

If you suspect that someone you care about is suffering from an anxiety disorder, the first thing you need to do is determine the role you want to play. This chapter focuses on how to do that. Along the way, it will talk about how to set boundaries and create a mental space that will help you help the person who is hurting.

Start by asking yourself some questions. How involved do you want to be? How much time can you give? What kind of help can you offer?

Before you can approach the person you care about, you also need to consider that person's point of view. Are you the right person to approach him about what is happening? Will she feel comfortable about your asking her how you can help? Is this something he could acknowledge to you? Has he acknowledged it to himself yet? More than that, does she realize she is suffering from anxiety and that it is something that can be treated? If not, would she listen to your suggestion that she be checked out?

These are important questions because the answers will dictate what you do next and how you do it. Just as you cannot be all things to all people, you cannot be all things to a person who is struggling with this illness. This is true whether you are a friend or acquaintance, a neighbor or coworker, a family member or someone who shares his home. Even if you have joined your lives together, in sickness and in health, this is not something you must do alone. You will want to become a member of a supportive group made up of people who care about the same person you care about.

It may be that you will take on the role of assembling that group. Some may have noticed the same things you have noticed and not known how to bring up the subject. They will be relieved and encouraged that you see what they see and that you have thought about ways for all of you to help.

The main thing is just to get started, to communicate with the person you care about and to form a network that can serve, at first, as a safety net and then as believers to help her move forward. The rest of this book will suggest the specific things you can do as keepers of the safety net, and as believers and sustainers, to help her face this thing and bring quality back to her life.

What if I'm far away?

Distance doesn't matter; caring does. You can provide encouragement and a place to vent through phone calls, e-mail, and with handwritten notes. You can consult with the other people who care about him. You can help her set up appointments for professional help. You can make your presence felt. You can give the person you care about the deep assurance that you can be depended on.

Burning out

If you have had a primary role in caring for someone who is ill, or have watched someone else carry out that role in the past, you know how much energy it takes and how depleting it can be. But it doesn't have to be that way.

It's important for you to think about this, because if you don't set some boundaries your effort could consume you. You need to know what you can and cannot do. You need to know that you can intensify your efforts at certain times and be less involved at others. You need to know you're not going it alone.

When you decide your role, when you enlist other people to form a supportive team, you decrease the chance of burnout. By setting boundaries you protect yourself and ensure that you will still live your life, still carry out your responsibilities, still maintain your other relationships, and continue to sustain and restore yourself. And when you do that, you will have the resilience to provide the best kind of help to the person who is suffering from anxiety.

Most important, you shouldn't feel locked into the decisions you make now. Circumstances can change. The ways in which you can help can change. The kind of support the person will welcome can change. And that means your role will change as it needs to.

SETTING BOUNDARIES

One way to set boundaries is to allocate different types of tasks or activities among the people who care, or arrange for some people to be available the first week of each month and others the second week, etc. Some people may prefer doing things *for* the person they care about, others may prefer doing things *with* him. Some people may be more comfortable with tasks, while others may be able to provide support through conversation. Some may be able to be on call to lend their strength during a panic attack while others would rather accompany a friend to a doctor's appointment.

Boundaries can also be set with the person you care about, and this can be done in a loving way.

You might say:

- "You can call anytime. Even if I can't talk at that minute, I will call you right back."
- "I know nighttime is hardest for you. Let me be the person you call in the middle of the night." Someone did that for me. Just knowing I could make that call if I needed to really helped.
- "Wednesdays are my flexible days. Anytime you need support on a Wednesday, I'm your man."
- "There are a number of errands I end up doing every week. It's no big deal to add to my grocery, mail, pharmacy, and banking lists. Just let me know."
- "Mornings are really tough for me because I'm trying to get out the door, and I'll be out on Saturdays since I committed my time to that association, but anytime after 6:00 p.m. on weekdays and all day Sunday, I can be there. Let's just try not to make it *every* weekday night or my boss might notice a lack of concentration!"
- "You know, we hardly ever spend time together anymore, so maybe we should set up a regular 'date' of sorts. How about if we plan on some sort of dinner every Thursday night? Nothing fancy, it could be takeout that we eat in."

PROTECTING YOURSELF

You can do little good if the person you care about doesn't sense positive feelings from you—empathy, caring, respect, commitment. On the other hand, if you get too deeply involved emotionally, you could begin to get traumatized yourself. So it's important to pay attention to your own reactions and to find a balance. You may need to back away sometimes to restore your own equilibrium and replenish yourself. If you are part of a network of people who care, many of you will find that there are times when you are more actively involved and times when you are less so. There will be an ebb and flow to this as there is to other things in life. And it is always okay to ask for help when you need it.

When it comes to personal relationships and comfort, detachment divides people and love unites them. So, for the person you care about who is suffering from anxiety, the more you distance yourself emotionally the harder it is for her. This means that striking a balance is not enough. When you need to distance yourself, or realize that you already have been doing so, you could lessen the blow by acknowledging it in some way.

You might say:

- "I've been feeling really overwhelmed lately. I think I need to take a couple of days to rest and recharge. I'm going to hole myself up in my room, shut the world out, read pulp fiction, watch TV, and sleep. But I'll be back next week."
- "I don't know how it happened exactly, but I'm so behind in everything that I feel as if I'm going to flip out. All my responsibilities just keep repeating in my mind. I'm going to take the next few days to try to clear some of that away."
- "I imagine you've noticed that I've been sort of distracted lately. My place looks like a tornado went through it, and I'm not sure what my kids are up to. I'm going to carve out some time to sort things out, so for the next week or so we may be talking on the phone more than getting together in person. I don't think it'll take too long."
- "We may laugh about this someday. You know how husbands and wives complain that their spouses aren't paying enough attention to them? Well, mine's on my case for not paying enough attention to *myself*. Made me promise to set

aside a week in which I'd do nothing but the most basic essentials—eat, sleep, go to work, cook dinner, and talk to him and the kids during dinner. No outings, no errands, no phone calls, no work brought home, no cleaning out closets, no setting up appointments, no evening meetings, no volunteer work, no traveling on business. For a whole week, all week! I know you won't find it surprising that there is no good week to do that. But I promised to commit to an entire week and that it would be one of the next four weeks, so will you help me pick one?"

WHAT ABOUT DEPENDENCY?

People suffering from anxiety respond to offers of help in a variety of ways. Some may have mixed feelings and vacillate between wanting help and not wanting help. They may feel embarrassed at needing it, or guilty about accepting it, or feel strongly about remaining independent. And you, too, may worry that too much help on your part could lead them to become overly dependent on you. That your help might actually turn out to be a hindrance that slows down the recovery process. So some people will push you away and some will seem to become overreliant on you and less able to function on their own. And the same person might do both.

Healing takes time, and while the process is going on, people will need a lot of help. Because injuries to the mind are invisible, it can be more difficult to grasp or anticipate what is needed than it might be with physical injuries. But people with anxiety need to relearn trust, and they often need to gain faith in others before they can gain faith in themselves. We hold out a hand to help someone across the street until he is ready to do it on his own, and we are prepared to do it many times over a long period of time because that is what it takes. This is similar. And in both cases, when the time is right, both you and he will want to gradually disengage. He will want separation and independence; you will take pride in his achievement.

But that could be a long way off. In the meantime, the way you think about what you are doing and the way you think about the person you care about can play a vital role in making a difference.

NURTURING A MINDSET

To be most supportive to the people we care about, we first have to communicate with ourselves. Just as we need to see through their eyes (the focus of the next chapter), we need to be sure of what we are seeing through *our* eyes. More than that, we need to take charge of our thoughts and put ourselves in a particular frame of mind—where we are consciously thinking of how much we respect the person who is suffering, how much we care for that person, how much it has meant that he cares for us, and how much we will do to respect her dignity. Taking the time to do this before spending time together will do more to promote their well-being than almost anything else you could do, and it will make everything else you say and do more effective.

This is because we all can sense how others feel about us, and we don't even need visual contact to do that. When we are in a telephone conversation, we can feel if the other person is really listening to what we are saying; we know when that person is thinking about something else at the same time, or doing something else—even when there is no sound to alert us. And other people can sense the same about us.

When we go to visit someone who cares about us, we can feel how much they anticipate being with us, the joy they expect, the pleasure because it is us—all before they utter a word. And that enhances our anticipation, our pleasure, and our confidence that they want to spend time with us and will listen attentively because they both love and respect us.

People suffering from anxiety do not lose this capacity to sense how others feel about them. If anything, anxiety may send their antennae up even higher. This is why we must keep in mind that no matter how tired, how worried, how frustrated we are when we see the people we care about struggling and suffering, we need to convey that we still see them as whole persons, and we still love and respect them as much as ever.

The beginning of doing that is to remind yourself of it, and to keep on reminding yourself. It will give weight to the words you say. It will give substance to the things you do. And it will give them the strength to persevere. When they can feel that you believe in them, they can work on restoring their belief in themselves.

CLEARING YOUR MIND

Just as you need to fill your mind with positive thoughts about the person you care about, you need to empty your mind of all the things that distract you. Things you still need to do today, places you need to go once you leave, the things that went wrong at work, the meeting you have scheduled for tomorrow. You have to make space for the positive thoughts.

SLOWING DOWN

You also have to make time count. The best way for time to feel full, complete, shared, productive, and longer than it is by the clock, is to be unrushed. And the best way to achieve that is to focus on the moment.

Try doing some deep breathing, or deliberately spend sixty seconds thinking about something you very much enjoy that always relaxes you. Maybe it's lying in bed with the Sunday newspaper, or watching boats sail across the water, or feeling the sun on your face, or melting from a back rub. Make sure it's sixty seconds and that you think of it that way—maybe even count to sixty as you do it. Sixty seconds going by one by one will feel much longer than a single minute.

And whether you are walking up to her home to visit, or walking towards your phone to call him, pay attention to the rhythm of your pace and cut it in half. Walking more slowly will slow the beat of your heart and the racing of your thoughts. This will help you be more attentive, a better listener, and a more profound speaker as you connect with the people you care about.

Your calm will help them.

GIVE THEM A CHANCE TO NURTURE YOU

Nurturing someone else is very powerful. It helps people feel connected; it gives their lives purpose; it confers dignity. There are things you can say that will make people realize they have this role in your life and that will give them a sense of well-being, if even for a moment. Note that these don't refer to anxiety at all. Sometimes it's better not to dwell there. Here are some suggestions:

- "I'm happy to see you."
- "No matter what, it always restores me to spend time with you."
- "Hey, it looks like this was a wearing day for you. Let's try to kick back a little."
- "It's so great to be here."
- "Okay with you if I just breathe for a few minutes?"
- "It's so relaxing that I don't have to put on an act for you."
- "Hi. Just wanted to hear your voice."

- "Someone's really set a pace today! Thought I'd take a breather and talk to you for a minute."
- "Hey, long time no hear. Are you hanging in?"
- "I need something to look forward to. Could we set a time to have coffee?"
- "I'd love to drop by. Would one night this week be okay?"

"Most words evolved as a description of the outside world, hence their inadequacy to describe what is going on inside me."

∂ Hugh Prather

Chapter Four

Seeing Through Their Eyes

෯

What Anxiety Feels Like

𝓘t's not easy to help people with something you haven't experienced yourself. Or, in this case, if you mistakenly assume you have experienced something similar just because it has the same name. Understanding what an anxiety disorder feels like, and gradually realizing how different this is, how overwhelming, how enormously life changing and life disrupting it is, will greatly add to your ability to help someone you care about who is suffering from it.

The best people to tell you what it feels like are the people who have experienced it. So this chapter brings you their words. They talk about what it feels like, what they've found helpful, what they've found makes it more difficult to cope. The focus is on what their friends and family can do to help, with some tips on what to avoid.

It's not the same for everyone, but by hearing what a number of different people—friends, clients, students, people I've worked with, and friends I've made while visiting people who are suffering—have said to me over the years, you will begin to get a sense of what anxiety feels like from the inside.

WHAT DOES ANXIETY FEEL LIKE?

- "I'm always on edge."
- "As if there's a rock in my gut."
- "This constant burning in my chest."
- "Just worried all the time."
- "Scared in my bones."
- "As if I can't breathe. Sometimes I can't get any air at all."
- "My heart pounds so hard it hurts."
- "As if my heart's going to break through my ribs."
- "My mind feels on fire."
- "Cold all the time."
- "Scared."
- "So worried I'm nauseous with it."
- "My mind won't stay still. It can't focus on anything else."
- "As if I have to spend all my time avoiding things and all my attention to protect myself."
- "Shaky. Trembling."
- "As if nothing will be right again."
- "As if I'm not an adult anymore. Just a sniveling wreck."
- "Spineless."
- "Incapable."
- "Consumed."
- "As if my life is permanently changed. As if my old life is over."
- "In constant dread."
- "Separated from people. Separated from places. Separated from activities."
- "Paralyzed and frenetic at the same time."
- "On constant alert."
- "As if an alarm is always going off in my head."
- "As if adrenaline keeps rushing and rushing, surging and surging, never shutting down."

- "Never safe. Something is always about to happen."
- "As if things aren't right."
- "Like I'm on the outside looking in."
- "It's hard to explain. It's surreal."
- "As if my body's gearing up in anticipation."
- "The sensation of having lost who I was as a person."
- "As if the person I was, the strength of character—the mental, emotional, intellectual capabilities just flew out the window."
- "Can't concentrate on anything, or organize anything, or read anything serious, or take in television news."
- "As if I'm shutting down, frozen. I can't move. I can't talk. Can't even get a sound out."
- "As if there's a giant rubber band being pulled tighter and tighter around my chest. It doesn't feel like rubber, though; it feels like steel."
- "As if I'm always letting people down."

HOW DOES IT AFFECT WHAT YOU DO?

- "I'm afraid of getting seriously involved with anyone or spending a lot of time with any one person because I don't want to risk what could happen when she finds out."
- "Every business trip is a nightmare because of the potential nightmare that could happen and because of all the planning that goes into trying to avoid it."
- "Vacations are much more stressful than ordinary life. I come back a wreck whether something happened or not. So I just don't go anymore."
- "It takes up my time. And a lot of thought and energy. I wish they could be spent on other things. How much better life could be; how much more I could accomplish; how much more fun I could have. It's tiring dealing with this."

- "I have to commit to less because I never know what I can live up to or even if I'll show up. I lose time. Sometimes the fear takes over and I just space out. I don't even know it until I come back to myself."
- "I'm always having to opt out or ask strange questions. It makes me seem odd or makes people feel I don't like them. Then they decide not to like me."
- "It makes me afraid of going places or being with people because I'm afraid of looking stupid or being rejected."

WHERE DOES IT SEEM TO COME FROM?

- "I don't know."
- "This kind of anxiety runs in my family."
- "I went through a really bad experience. Can't seem to recover from it. It touches everything."
- "Never was afraid of this before. Then, suddenly, at the worst possible moment, this terror came out of nowhere. It paralyzed me. And it's stuck to me; I can't get rid of it."
- "I'm starting to learn what sets it off, but I don't know what started it in the first place."

WHAT KIND OF SUPPORT HELPS THE MOST?

- "Patience."
- "Staying with me."
- "Standing by me."
- "Showing you still respect me."
- "Listening to what I say about how I feel."
- "Respecting my understanding of myself—my capabilities, my limitations."
- "Working with me to manage my life."
- "Recognizing that I could be suffering from an illness."
- "Working with me to get help."

- "Supporting me while I get it."
- "Understanding that they don't know how it feels."
- "Wanting to spend time with me anyway."
- "Helping me focus on other things."
- "Giving me temporary relief by finding ways to distract me."
- "Understanding if I need to be alone, if I need quiet."
- "Understanding how on edge I am, that the least little agitation could be a last straw."
- "Recognizing that sometimes the only distraction is doing something mindless."
- "Calling when they say they will. Sometimes it's the only thing that gets me through."
- "Not expecting me to heal on some sort of schedule."
- "Recognizing that this is real."
- "Not expecting a happy face all the time. Letting me be me."

WHAT HURTS? GETS IN THE WAY? SETS ME BACK?

- "Insisting that this is all in my head."
- "Pushing me to do things I can't do."
- "Getting angry at me for being weak."
- "Insisting that other people get over this."
- "Thinking they know what it feels like."
- "Talking about times when they've been nervous and how they overcame it. Insisting it's the same thing."
- "Resisting the idea that this could be an illness."
- "Getting angry when I don't pull myself together."
- "Getting angry that it's taking me so long."
- "Calling me ridiculous for giving up activities I used to enjoy."
- "Suggesting I call when I'm back to 'normal.'"
- "Saying they wish they could just shake me."
- "Saying a good shock would snap me out of it."
- "Judging me."

- "Ignoring me."
- "Refusing to see that I'm suffering."
- "Talking to me about it all the time. Sometimes I'd rather not talk about it."
- "Patronizing me as if I'm something less."
- "Pitying me."
- "Thinking I don't want to get well."

WHAT WOULD YOU SAY TO FAMILY AND FRIENDS WHO TRY TO HELP?

- "Sometimes your support is the only thing that gets me through the day."
- "You make me feel there's hope."
- "You refuel my strength."
- "You make me feel like a person."
- "When I need to talk about it, you listen. You really listen."
- "I feel so alone in this. It helps when you are there, even if you don't talk."
- "You talk to me like you always did. It pulls me out for a while."
- "Just knowing you are there. That you'll come. That you'll call. That I can call you. It means so much."
- "The people who stand by you, who respect you, they make all the difference."
- "There are so few people I can confide in when I'm going through this. You are one of the few."
- "I may not be able to tell you, and I may be difficult and show resentment, but I know you care and it does help— more than I could ever explain."

Part II

❧

WORDS MATTER
What to Say

"Words may be deeds."

⇛ Aesop

Chapter Five

Opening the Conversation

༃

FIRST THINGS TO SAY

*I*f you suspect that someone you care about is suffering from anxiety, it may not be easy to jump in and say it. Even if you are very close, this is still something you may want to lead up to. This chapter suggests some ways to show your concern so that the person you care about will be more likely to welcome your support and talk with you about what is happening.

You could start by checking in with them generally, mentioning things you have noticed. You could gradually bring up the fact that you are concerned about them, that what you have been seeing seems to be happening more and more.

"Gradually" is a good watchword to use. Don't hit them with everything at once, or even in the same conversation. Take things one step at a time. Find times over a period of weeks where you can bring up your concerns. Give them a chance to realize that you care and continue to care. That maybe they could trust you with what they are feeling, what is happening to them. If you crowd them, this is less likely to happen.

And eventually, you may be able to suggest that they seek professional advice.

Start with a question

- "Everything okay? You don't seem quite yourself."
- "I've missed seeing you around. Hope you're going to be around more."
- "You seem a little on edge lately. Can I give you a hand with anything?"
- "I've been a little on edge lately. Are you feeling that way, too?"
- "We seem to have lost touch the last couple of weeks. How are things with you?"

Make observations

- "You've been missing a lot of get-togethers lately. What's up?"
- "Over the past few weeks you've been late almost every day. This isn't like you. What's going on?"
- "You've been missing work at least one day a week for weeks now. And the other days you've barely made it in by lunch. What happened?"
- "Have I done something wrong? You never return phone calls anymore. Someone else mentioned not hearing from you either. Can we talk about it?"
- "You've turned down the last three excursions. Hiking used to be your favorite thing. Did something happen last time? Would you rather try a new activity?"

Express concern

- "I feel like I'm butting in, but we've been friends for a long time. Something's wrong. Please tell me how to help."

- "I don't want you to start avoiding my phone calls, but I'm really worried that you never want to go anywhere anymore. The last time we did something was about six weeks ago, and I have this weird feeling that you haven't gone anywhere since. Have you?"
- "I've known you for a long time. I can tell when something's got you churned up. I don't think I've ever seen you this uptight. It's scaring me, and I think it's scaring you."
- "Maybe I'm exaggerating a little, but somehow I don't think I am. Something has you spooked. I'd really like to get down to specifics so we can work on this together—figure out what's going on and how to fix it."
- "Whatever is going on is bleeding you of energy and keeping you from all the things you like to do. Let's just tackle it the way we have other problems we've had."

LET THEM TAKE THE LEAD

- "I'm ready to talk about this whenever you are."
- "I'd like to help you with this. I know you would help me."
- "I don't know if I'm part of the problem, but I hope you'll let me be part of the solution."
- "It's really hard for me to stand by and see you suffer. Please let me help with whatever this is."
- "I hope you know I'll be there whenever you want me. I just hope you won't wait too long because you don't deserve to suffer like this."
- "I know you're trying to cope with this in your own way; just know I'm available and want to help if I can."

TREAT THEM WITH RESPECT

- "You're a great person. Whatever this is, we're going to get past it."
- "You know yourself better than anyone. You call the shots."
- "You're a very strong person, but no one is Superman. Whatever is getting to you, I could never think less of you."
- "I know it's a terrible cliché, but sometimes two heads really are better than one. If you think I can help, just let me know. I'll be here."
- "Don't forget you have some really good friends (which is not surprising because you are a really good friend yourself). I know I'd be glad to help you with whatever is going on. I don't want to intrude, though, and I figure everyone else probably feels the same way. They may just be waiting for the slightest sign from you that they would be welcome."
- "Hey, I miss you. If you're too busy with work, maybe I can free you up somewhere so you can get it done. Or if you're having a problem, maybe I can help you with it. If it's illness, I hope you won't push me away. If something's frightening you, maybe I can help brainstorm what to do about it. Whatever it is, I value you and I value our friendship. Nothing could change that."
- "No matter how horrible this is, or how mundane, or how silly, or how embarrassing, it's not going to matter to me. I'm still going to think you're great. Maybe a little more human (just kidding)."
- "I have always trusted that you would be there for me. I'd like to be there for you."

What is most important is to let them know you are there. That you care, you will listen, and you will help. That you respect them entirely and will respect how they want to proceed.

Focus more on making statements than asking questions. Or on asking questions in such a way that they don't have to say very much in reply. They may not be able to respond now, but when they are ready to talk, they will feel assured that you will listen and trust you not to come in and just take over. This is important, because they already have the feeling of having been taken over. What they need now is someone who can support them, who believes in them, who can become a partner in this war that's wearing them down.

Down the road you can ask more specific questions, or push for answers. Initially, though, it's better to ask questions that have ordinary polite responses (such as "I'm fine," "Things are okay," "Thanks for asking," "A little hectic," "Just fighting a cold"), or to make comments that don't require any answer at all. This gives people a choice—to use the opening you are giving them or not to. And it does so in a way that isn't threatening or embarrassing. You don't want them to feel put on the spot because that might increase their stress and anxiety. You want to give them the feeling that they can come to you and increase the likelihood that they will use the next opening you give them.

*"How does one kill fear, I wonder?
How do you shoot a spectre through the heart, slash
off its spectral head, take it by its spectral throat?"*

— Joseph Conrad

Chapter Six

Words That Wobble

ༀ

GIVING IT A NAME

Once you have realized that someone you care about may be suffering from anxiety and have decided to approach them about it, you should be prepared to say the word "anxiety" and explain what it is. This is important, and this chapter explains why.

We use words to nail things down. In giving something a name, we feel we have defined it. Said what it is as well as what it is not. We may even feel we gain some control over the thing we have named.

And this feeling matters. Once we give something a name, we feel we know what we are dealing with. We feel we can talk about it with someone else and they will know what we mean. We can dismiss it, or plan around it, or aim for it.

We do this with objects, with people, with activities; we do this with emotions, and we do it with our dreams.

When we put a dream into words, it becomes real, something tangible that we can aim for. We can start to plan for it and take concrete steps towards it.

Similarly, when we name an emotion or a fear, we can become more objective about it. Distance ourselves from it a bit. Begin to believe it is only a part of who we are, not all of who we are. And that is the first step in managing it—in being able to control it rather than have it control us.

The same is true when we feel someone we love is struggling. If we know what they are struggling against, if we can give it a name, we are in a better position to help.

The more distinct the word is, the easier it is to do these things. And that's where the rub is when someone is suffering from anxiety, because the word "anxiety" isn't very solid around the edges. At least not in the way we generally use it.

Because we use it to cover temporary, everyday kinds of things such as nervousness before an exam, butterflies before a speech, stage fright before a performance, jitters before meeting a new boss or prospective in-laws, it can be difficult to remember that it is also used clinically to cover more intense, longer-lasting, extreme forms of anxiety that get in the way of everyday functioning. "Anxiety" covers a whole range of disorders, each with its own separate clinical name based on what it looks like or on the functioning with which it interferes.

We need to be willing to explore the possibility that this is what the person we care about is struggling with because he may not realize that there is a difference between everyday anxiety and clinical anxiety. He may think he is weak in letting fear take over. She may think her nervousness is all her fault. They may not know they could be suffering from an illness that is treatable.

Or they may be afraid to give it a name. And sometimes, we, too, are afraid to give something a name. We think that by acknowledging it by name we give it more power. Actually, the opposite is true. When we don't give it a name, we give it free range. When we name it, we limit its power. We set it in its place and set ourselves against it. We create space in which a battle can take place. No longer is it a murky, shapeless, shape-changing force that can come at one from all sides.

Don't let it be a nightmare with no name. When anxiety is tied down by what you call it, then it is possible to get help—to know what kind of help is needed, where to go to get it, and what you can do yourself.

"*Reason explains the darkness,
but it is not a light.*"

⌇ NOAH benShea

Chapter Seven

Words That Hurt

ॐ

What Not to Say

*B*ecause of the way life is, we all have some experience in comforting the people we care about, in providing words of advice, words of encouragement, and words of cheer. Some of those words can come to our lips almost automatically because they are formulaic in nature, words we've heard others use and find ourselves repeating. However, as helpful as these stock phrases can be in usual situations, they can be surprisingly unhelpful when someone is suffering from an anxiety disorder. They can even hurt, and they can increase the anxiety.

The next chapter will focus on words that help, but first it is important to understand what not to say. So this chapter gives examples of phrases to look out for and discusses some of the reasons why they can end up doing the opposite of what you intended. Often, it's because the person you care about hears something quite different from what you mean.

As you look over these examples and see why they can boomerang, you will get a feeling for what phrases can work and what phrases won't, and you'll become comfortable developing your own things to say.

"I KNOW WHAT YOU'RE GOING THROUGH."

You are trying to show empathy, that you know this is painful and frightening, and you are with her, but it doesn't come across that way. Instead it can come across as a need to talk about yourself or a jumping to the conclusion that the two experiences are the same and that the solutions will be the same. When one is in this kind of pain, though, it feels unique, and one doesn't want to hear about someone else's experience.

Even when you've suffered from anxiety yourself, even if you've suffered from the same form of anxiety, it doesn't help to say this. Not only because anxiety is different for everyone, but because each time someone goes through it, it's different for that individual, too. The way it feels, how it came on, how intense, the context, and the details surrounding it will vary. These episodes don't come from a cookie cutter.

"I THINK YOU'RE OVERREACTING."

You're only trying to help, to calm him down, but that is not what he hears. On one level, he already knows he is overreacting, and he is embarrassed about it. Your underscoring this makes him think that you are embarrassed by his behavior or that you want to make sure that he realizes that *he should* feel embarrassed. This can only make him feel worse and may even cause his anxiety to increase.

On another level, overreacting is a part of the illness and something he can't control. So what he hears is that you don't understand the illness or his behavior, and that you seem to think he can control his reaction at this particular moment. He thinks you think less of him.

"Relax."

Just as we can't fall in love on command, we can't relax on command. Not at someone else's command, not even at our own. When we are upset and someone tells us to relax, we often will become more tense, more angry, more upset. This is a natural reaction because it feels as if what we are upset about doesn't seem important to the other person or because the way we feel doesn't seem warranted to that person.

When a person is suffering from anxiety, she may even have an unspoken—maybe even unconscious—wish that the other person will share her feeling of being upset or be upset on her behalf. So if you tell the person you care about to relax, she may feel that you are talking down to her, or even that you are not on her side. On an unconscious level, she may feel betrayed as well as saddened.

Simply letting her know you'll be there with her while she is feeling this way is much more likely to help her gradually relax.

"Try not to tense up all the time. Try not to think about being tense."

It would be wonderful if our saying this would work, yet more often it will backfire. It's very difficult to erase a thought after someone else has emphasized it in this way, and it's very difficult to block out a feeling. This is especially true when someone tells us *not* to feel something; if we are already feeling it, telling us not to will only intensify the feeling.

"I know you have self-discipline."

You mean this in a very positive way, but the way you say it can make it seem very negative.

If you say this without qualifying it in some way, she may think that you think self-discipline is all it will take to conquer this. Or she may think that you don't understand why she hasn't drawn on it. Or that you think she brought the anxiety on herself, or that it is her responsibility to put this aside and she is shirking it. And she will view herself as weak, flawed, lazy, and diminished in your eyes.

If, on the other hand, you say that no matter how hard this is going to be, and how long it takes to get well, that the self-discipline she has always had will be something she can bring to the battle that will help her get through this, then you are offering her a strength. You are saying the anxiety is not her fault or the sum of who she is, but something that is hurting her. And that you still see the whole of who she is.

"YOU'RE WORRYING ABOUT NOTHING."

You are trying to give him perspective, and under ordinary circumstances that might help. But this "worry" is part of a disease process and though his mind knows this shouldn't be a big deal, he can't help his reactions. For him, it *is* a big deal and it is hurtful and scary and is interfering with his life. The scariest part is that he can't make it stop, and the most hurtful part is that the people around him either dismiss it because they don't understand it or act as if they think he is crazy.

Part of him may want to scream back at you, "Of course I know it is nothing! What difference does that make?"

The thing is, it isn't just "worry." It's anxiety. And that is a very powerful force. The usual rules don't apply.

"JUST DO IT."

When we are a little nervous, a little push and the confidence of those around us can sometimes help us do a thing we didn't think we could do. But when someone is terrified, a little push won't work and can backfire. The person suffering from anxiety could end up traumatized and less likely to ever tackle it in the future.

Anxiety can produce terror and generate panic attacks. It can make people freeze in dangerous situations, which can endanger them even more. You may think that with a little push and your confidence behind them that they will be able to act. That by dwelling on their fear they only increase it, and that by facing their fear it will immediately dissipate. With everyday fears and nervousness this can work. With anxiety, even a systematic approach and a trained professional can take a long time to achieve results. Relief doesn't come right away.

When you say this to someone you care about, and they can't "just do it," they will feel they've let *you* down as well as themselves. They will feel your disappointment, assume you are angry, and fear that you won't be bothered with them anymore. Those few words, like a pebble in a pond, will generate more ripples than you ever dreamed.

"IT'LL BE FINE."

You may want this to be true and for the person you care about to believe it, but to the person you say this to, this is just another form of imposing expectations that they don't think they will ever meet.

These are words you might say as you ask someone with social phobia to attend a party with you, or that you say to someone with OCD when you want him to be satisfied he has completed one step of a ritual and is ready to move on to the next one. But when they can't bring themselves to go, they know—and they know you know—that it isn't fine. That they are not fine. And every time this happens they feel as if maybe it will never be fine again. Unfortunately, sometimes your caring words of encouragement—even your tenderness—can be interpreted as something else. Because they are impatient and frustrated with themselves, they think you are impatient and frustrated with them.

"You'll see, it will go away as suddenly as it came."

This is unlikely, and people suffering from anxiety can't help but know this. They realize you want to inspire them and encourage them, and that you struggle for the right things to say as they would if your positions were reversed. But they also realize that, as they are suffering and struggling and feeling invaded and frightened, they have come to value truth more and more. You don't mean to lie to them. In fact, you feel that when they turn a corner, no matter how long it takes, all of a sudden they *will* feel free and empowered. But that is not what this sounds like. It sounds like the anxiety will disappear—*poof*—with the sweep of a wand, and that everything will be as it was before.

Your respect for them as whole people is very important to them. That it persist in spite of illness, anxiety, mistakes, and other vicissitudes of life. Truth is one of the pillars of the respect between friends, and they need to be able to trust what you are telling them. Because, as someone's life narrows to the bare essentials, truth becomes something stark and visible.

What are some other things to avoid?

- Offering advice unless he asks for it.
- Saying the same thing over and over, as if you require a response. (She may not wish to acknowledge what you said for any number of reasons: not wanting to explain herself,

not wanting to get into an argument, not wanting you to feel bad, not having the energy, not wanting to go over territory you have already covered.)

- Saying the same thing in a louder and louder or more and more emphatic voice, as if his lack of response means he didn't hear you. Anxiety does not confer deafness. You may be trying to get his attention, trying to get him to focus on what you are saying. He, on the other hand, may feel a lack of respect because this is how we sometimes treat children (which means you don't see him as an adult), or speak to nonnative speakers (as if deafness comes along with fluency in a different tongue), or compensate when speaking to people who are elderly (as if stupidity is a part of hearing loss).

- Arguing with her about what you meant when she misinterprets what you say. If what you say goes over badly, apologize and move on. Arguing will only increase stress for both of you and the misunderstanding could deepen.

"*There is no calamity that right words will not begin to redress.*"

—ᴿᴬᴸᴾᴴ ᵂᴬᴸᴰᴼ ᴱᴹᴱᴿˢᴼᴺ

Chapter Eight

Words That Help

What to Say

*P*eople suffering from anxiety are being flooded with negative images of the world, with threats to their composure and their lives, with negative views of themselves. Their whole thought process may have changed. In a way, their minds have taken "the glass is half-empty" perspective to extremes. To them, it *is* empty—of hope, of faith, of possibility. There is no room for dreams because they can't come true, especially those dreams of feeling safe and not having to worry all the time.

What you want to do is add something to that glass. Water it, as you would a garden. And, to mix metaphors even more, color it rose. No one should have to always look at the world through shadows.

This chapter suggests some things to say—positive things the person you care about may not absorb right away, but that can float around in her mind with all those negative thoughts and eventually connect with something. Maybe she'll focus on them sometimes. Maybe each one will glom on to a negative thought and slow it down or neutralize it, as antibodies do to germs. Maybe they'll cling together and form a fighting force that grows ever larger. Maybe they'll just take up space so fewer negative thoughts can gather.

Thinking about them in this way can become a positive force for you as well as for the person you care about. Recent studies indicate that prayer and faith make a measurable difference in people's recoveries from all sorts of illnesses, even when they aren't told of it. There is a lot of visualization in prayer. But it can also help *you* to visualize what might be happening with the words you send out into their world. You send words with love and with pain, with hope and with fear. You convert your energy into something you hope will help to transform the people you care about, help them to transform and heal themselves. Yet you seldom see that your words have landed to live in their hearts. You can wait months to see seeds bear fruit. And you can never know the exact part your contributions played. But your visualizations can, and they can sustain you as you try to support the people in your life who are suffering.

Here are a few examples of things to say that can help.

"I WISH THIS WEREN'T HAPPENING TO YOU."
This statement makes no judgments. It tells those suffering from anxiety that you don't see this as their fault and you don't think it is something they did to themselves. That you care about them and wish life hadn't sent them this to deal with. Most important, it tells them that you still see them as the same people they always have been. This will make it possible for them to talk to you and will make it easier for them to accept your help, because this statement implies respect.

"I CAN SEE HOW INCREDIBLY HARD THIS IS."
This, too, implies respect—a respect that verges on awe. It shows that you recognize that this isn't some little hill that must be climbed, but a mountain that will need to be scaled with all that modern science and technology, careful preparation, physical

and psychological toughening, and experienced professionals can provide. This statement shows that you recognize the immense challenge and respect what she will be facing.

"LET'S TREAT THIS AS WE WOULD ANY OTHER ILLNESS."

Because people with anxiety fear that others think they are crazy, or that they exaggerate their fears, or that they are unwilling to take control of their own minds, they expect to be treated like lepers or at least with disdain. With this statement, you don't push anxiety into some corner; you are saying you don't make distinctions among illnesses. You show your conviction that this is a challenge that can be met. And you suggest that the two of you think of this as something treatable, something to learn about, something to get professional help with, something to deal with so he can get on with his life.

And when you say this, you shore up his self-respect and reassure him that your relationship is intact and won't be damaged by this. That it might even be strengthened.

"LET'S DO SOMETHING TO GET OUR MINDS OFF IT."

This statement brings perspective. It shows that you see anxiety as you see other things that can take over a person's life, bring her down, consume her thoughts and energy, and that you see ignoring it once in a while as a healthy thing to do. You put things back in the realm of normalcy, and by doing that you show you haven't put her in some other category.

You are also acknowledging and accepting that some things don't go away easily or quickly. That if that's the way it is, even if you'd both rather it be otherwise, it is okay and you can deal with it. That if she were dealing with overwork, or grief, or family problems or something chronic, you would encourage her to allow herself breaks and distractions. That anxiety is no different and she deserves to find fun where she can.

"Please tell me how to help."

It's not only important not to judge, it's important to reinforce your belief in his good judgment. When you ask someone how to help, you are saying you don't understand much about anxiety and you won't pretend to because you haven't experienced it firsthand. At the same time, you are saying that you want to help and you are ready to be told what to do and to be directed in how to do it. That shows respect.

"I'll be there for you; we'll get through this."

More than anything, people suffering from anxiety need to know they are not alone, and that you still see them as equals. This statement tells them that. The first part assures them of your support and your presence. By using the word "we" in the second part, you emphasize that you are peers, partners, a team facing this together. And that, of course, this is stuff no one should go through alone.

"I wish I'd known before; I could have helped you sooner."

Offering your help retroactively as well as promising it into the future is more than reassuring, it is redeeming. It means that this is what friends are for and that you consider yourself one. It means that you don't see any shame in her suffering from anxiety. It just is. It's just hard. And you're not going anywhere.

"I always knew you were an amazing person. I just never knew how amazing!"

Validation can generate strength, calm, and energy. When you tell them that you see them as even more than you saw them before, that knowing they are struggling with this actually increases your respect for them, they will feel such gratitude. Just when they are thinking less of themselves, and seeing those same thoughts reflected in other people's eyes and actions, and finding themselves scared and depleted so much of the time, that is just when they need to hear this. And this validation is truth—taking on something this tough this well takes an incredible person. They can't recognize it themselves so it's important that they hear it.

"I'M HAPPY TO HELP YOU ANY WAY I CAN. AND THAT INCLUDES FINDING SOME KNOWLEDGEABLE HELP. JUST LET ME KNOW. ANYTIME."

Just leaving the door open so they can feel comfortable approaching you later can feel like a breath of fresh air. They may already have been subjected to a lot of pressure from a lot of people, so a warm, flexible approach will be appreciated.

"I'M REALLY CONCERNED ABOUT YOU. I FEEL I WOULD BE FAILING YOU IF I DIDN'T SUGGEST YOU SEE A PROFESSIONAL."

How to encourage someone suffering from anxiety to seek treatment depends on your relationship with her and the severity of what you see. Broach the subject gently and in the form of a suggestion. Let her know that you are not judging her—you are trying to help because you care. Point out that if he had cancer or exhibited stroke symptoms, you would probably have hauled him off to see someone who could assess the situation and help. If this has been going on for some time, and he seems to be getting worse, it's okay to say that you are frustrated and that you surely wouldn't let him walk around with a high fever for days on end and this seems comparable.

"It's not easy, is it?"

We say this often, one adult to another, as we comment on life's other curves, or on life situations we have in common, such as dieting, workplace issues, and parenting teens when they're withdrawn or moody. The key is the camaraderie, the shared empathy, the one-adult-to-another nature of the comment. It offers the connection that comes from agreement, and an opening to take the conversation further.

"Man makes holy what he believes as he makes beautiful what he loves."

∽ ERNEST RENAN

Chapter Nine

Do's and Don'ts

⊰⊱

A Helpful Reference

*T*his chapter offers an overview of things that are helpful to say and do, and things that can be hurtful. The idea is not to prescribe exactly what to say, but to help you derive the principles underlying both groups so you can feel comfortable developing your own words. In addition, this chapter can also serve as a quick and easy reference.

When you're talking to someone suffering from anxiety, there are a couple of other things to keep in mind. First, don't argue feelings; argue facts. Best of all, don't argue, but range yourself on his side.

Second, focus on feeling and caring, rather than on orders and rules. For example, avoid saying "You ought to," "You should," "You need to," and instead say "I want you to," "I'd really like you to," and "I wish you would."

Third, make sure that what you say assures them of your respect and their inherent dignity. Don't push, prod, or mock them; don't show pity, disdain, or disrespect. Don't challenge them to do something they can't do, talk about them as if they are not there, or publicize their situation to someone else. Instead, focus on the things that work, find things to do that are comfortable, and remind them of all the things not affected by the anxiety. Above all, be patient and interact with them as if they were the same people they always have been—because they are.

DON'T SAY:	DO SAY:
Don't worry.	I know you worry.
Don't worry so much.	It's scary, isn't it?
Get over it.	How can I help?
Just do it.	Let's do it together.
You're weak.	You've shown such strength, but no one should have to do this alone.
Have some self-respect.	I have so much respect for you.
Of course you can do it.	This is really hard, isn't it?
I know you can do it.	Maybe not today, but I know you'll be able to do this eventually.
You were always able to do this before.	What's getting in the way?
What am I going to do about you?	How can we work on this together?
But we always enjoyed this!	What should we do instead?

You can't go on like this.	You can't be alone in this. Let's find out more about what's happening here.
Forget about the past.	I know you can't forget the past; I wouldn't ask you to.
I've never seen anything like this. You're crazy.	There is nothing unique under the sun. Let's find out what this is. I'll help.
This is nuts. Shake it off. Get yourself under control.	I know you're not doing this on purpose. Let's find out how other people get through this.
I don't even know you anymore.	This is happening to you. It is *not* you. We're going to figure out how to get control over it.
What's happening to you?	You're a fantastic person. We're not going to let this beat you down.
What are you so scared of?	This must be scary. I know I would find it scary.
You're stuck in this place. I'm not going to get stuck there with you!	Hey, do you feel as if you're getting stuck? I bet this has happened to thousands of other people. If it's okay with you, I'm going to find out what they do to get unstuck.

DON'T SAY:	DO SAY:
All you have to do is get back on the horse!	Don't worry. We'll figure this out. Besides, we need an easygoing horse, not a bucking bronco.
I just don't have patience for this!	You'll be ready when you're ready. It's okay.
I need you to be okay, so would you please just get on with it.	I know you get scared and frustrated and angry about this yourself. So do I sometimes. Let's just bear with each other, okay?
Just try it once.	It's no big deal. We don't have to do this.
It won't bite.	There's no reason to stay here. Let's get out of here.
It's just a matter of getting used to it, you'll see.	Why don't we do something else.
There's no reason to be scared.	You're safe. Let me hold you. (Make sure he is comfortable about being touched. Ask first.)
It's all in your mind.	Everyone's unnerved by something.

"*We can do no great things, only small things with great love.*"

꙳ MOTHER TERESA

Chapter Ten

When They Ask Questions

꒳

How to Respond

*M*iscommunication can happen in both directions. Just as others can misinterpret what *you* say, so can you misinterpret what *they* say. Chapter 7, Words That Hurt, focused on the first—how someone you care about can hear something very different from what you intended. This chapter focuses on the second—what you might miss when someone suffering from anxiety talks to you, and how that can affect your response.

We have been conditioned to answer a question by responding to what is explicitly being said when someone makes a comment. But sometimes, when we try to respond to the content, we may miss what someone is really saying, and we may miss what he is looking for.

We need to listen for what lies underneath the words. What is the emotion behind what he has said? What is she feeling? What does he want to feel?

Often, the person we care about is experiencing a negative emotion and looking for a positive one. She could be feeling uncertainty, despair, fear, confusion, or a feeling that she can't handle anything more. He might be looking for reassurance, hope, a shoulder to lean on, caring. They both want stable ground to walk on, the sense that they are not alone, and our conviction that they are not crazy or going crazy.

To help guide you, here are some things they might say and some suggestions of what you might say in return.

"I DON'T KNOW WHAT TO DO! WHAT CAN I DO?"

- "It's scary, isn't it?"
- "I don't know, but I'm going to help you find out."
- "I'd be scared, too. And I'd feel so alone. But you don't need to do this alone."
- "I wish I knew more about this. What have you found out so far? Maybe I could help you build on that."
- "I don't know, but I don't want you to have to go on suffering like this. Would it be okay with you if I asked around to see if there's someone you could talk to in strict confidence?"
- "I'm honored that you've asked me. Will you trust me to look into it?"

"I CAN'T GO. HOW DO I GET OUT OF IT?"

- "It's kind of overwhelming, isn't it?"
- "Did you accept already? If not, just say you can't make it. You don't have to explain."
- "If you've changed your mind, just say you can't make it after all. And if they ask you why, just say how sorry you are that you can't be there."
- "Would it help if I went with you?"
- "Maybe you need to know more about it before you can consider going. Give yourself some breathing room. You could tell them your plans for that week are still up in the air, but you hope you'll be able to work it out. Or ask what

the dress code will be or if there's anything you could plan on bringing. The conversation may turn up more details that way. If not, maybe I could find out more about the location or the plans or how crowded it will be or if you would know everyone. Maybe I could help you find out what it is that would make it feel safe. Would that help?"

- "Just say you'd like a rain check."

"I CAN'T HANDLE SURPRISES. CAN YOU CHECK FOR ME?"

- "I don't want you to be taken by surprise either. What should I check for?"
- "It's pretty nerve-racking having to wonder. I'll be happy to check it out."
- "Just leave it to me. I'll get you a full report."
- "I'll see what I can find out. If I can't get what you need, we can just skip it."

"THIS IS PARALYZING ME. WHY IS IT GETTING WORSE?"

- "I don't know, but I don't think you should let it keep going like this. What do you think?"
- "This isn't just scaring you, it's scaring me. I think it might be a good idea to get a check-up to see if you have a low mineral count or if something else is out of whack physically or chemically. Maybe we're just not seeing it and a doctor would catch it right away."
- "Maybe the fact it's getting worse just proves that there's something medically wrong. I think you should consider telling your doctor what has been happening. If you're not comfortable with the one you have, we can ask around and find someone else."

- "I think you've been battling this on your own long enough. Don't you feel the same way? Let's find someone who's seen this kind of thing before."

"WHAT MAKES YOU THINK YOU CAN UNDERSTAND?"

- "The only thing I understand is that you're hurting and it hurts me to see you this way."
- "I wish I did understand, because then I might be of more help."
- "I know I don't understand. Teach me what you know about it."
- "I'm angry at myself for not knowing more, and I think you are angry at me yourself for not knowing more. Please help me understand."
- "I'd be angry, too, if I were in your shoes. Angry at the whole world for continuing to spin when I'm so scared and it doesn't even make sense."

"I KNOW THIS ISN'T NORMAL. I'VE NEVER BEEN NORMAL. DON'T YOU REALIZE YOU JUST NEVER SAW IT BEFORE?"

- "You are one of the most normal people I know. This one thing doesn't change that, no matter how crazy-making it is."
- "Just because you never let me see this side of you doesn't mean I haven't seen a whole lot of other sides. And I like those other sides! If it's in your way, let's figure out what to do about it, that's all."
- "You say that because you are going through a bad patch. Because maybe you still never intended for me to see it. And

it's making you frustrated and angry. Do you think every-thing about *me* is normal through and through?"

- "It must be awful to have carried this around with you for so long, not saying anything to anyone and worrying about it all the time. But it can't be as bad as you think because I'm not running away from you screaming! Right?"

- "The more you try to swallow something, the bigger it seems to get. It's stuck in your throat. But now that I've seen some of it, why not get the rest of it out? If it's a secret, it's safe with me."

- "If you were completely normal, you probably wouldn't want me for a friend. But if this is something you want to change, tell me how to help."

- "I'm not sure if you are angry or sad or feeling exposed or not sure if you can trust me or something else. But I'm your friend, and I want to always be your friend. Even if you were to do something I didn't like, even if it were something ter-rible, even if I didn't like you very much for a while for hav-ing done it, it wouldn't change how I feel about you. I love the person you are, the whole you."

"I'm tired of hiding and pretending. Can't you just let me be?"

- "Yes! That is all I ever wanted."
- "I want you to be you. You don't have to pretend anything for me."
- "Removing barriers brings us closer. When you remove yours, it makes it easier for me to remove mine."
- "When you trust me like this I am so moved I could cry. Thank you."

- "It must take so much energy to hide and pretend all the time. I'd be angry, too, if I had to be on guard so much."
- "I would never ask you to reveal anything you don't want to. But if you could share whatever you're comfortable with sharing, that would allow me to help you. You can trust me."
- "I'm not sure what you are asking. If you are saying you are entitled to your privacy and want me to stop asking a million questions, and stop forcing you to weave half truths, I can respect that, because I respect you. If you are saying that you've been putting up a front all this time and that it's been hard work, but now you are ready to let me know more of you and hope I'll still like you, warts and all, then go for it. It'll just make you more interesting, give you more dimension. I already sense you are a complex person with many facets. I hope you'll want to know mine, too. There is always more to be revealed and the relationship just gets richer."
- "I'm sorry you haven't felt you could come to me with this before, but so glad you are now. Did you think I'd think less of you? I've always been proud of all you are and of all you've done. Now I'm even more proud to think you had this to contend with and still are a beautiful person. You don't have to do any hiding or pretending on my account."

"Let's get real here. Obviously, I'm unbalanced or crazy or something. What are you still hanging around for?"

- "This doesn't change anything for me, except maybe to make me proud to know you."
- "Please don't push me away. I'm not planning to go anywhere."

- "You are one of the most rational people I have ever known. Something is causing this thing and we're going to get to the bottom of it."
- "It must have been pretty scary to walk around with this thing. And pretty scary to wonder how people would react to it if you told them about it or they noticed something different. A broken leg or failing kidney or sudden mood swings wouldn't change what I think of you, so why should this?"
- "You must be scared, and the scariest thing must be not knowing what this is. I think you'd feel a lot better if you could put a name to it. I'd like to help you with that, if it's all right with you?"

"You've got your nerve. Haven't you heard of an eccentric before?"

- "Actually, I wish there were more eccentrics. They make life interesting, and it seems to me that there used to be a lot more of them. Or maybe they're just not as visible because people don't seem to appreciate eccentricity as much anymore."
- "If that's what this is, then I'm sorry to have intruded. I was worried that it might be something more. If it is, or you are concerned it might be, and I can help in some way, I hope you'll tell me."
- "You're a great guy and I'm sorry if I've done something to offend you."
- "You took me by surprise, and that's what you saw—surprise. If you don't want me to mention it, I won't. I don't have a problem with seeing another side of you; I'm just sorry that you are uncomfortable with it."

"YOU ASK TOO MANY QUESTIONS. HOW ABOUT TELLING ME ABOUT *YOUR* QUIRKS?"

- "You're just trying to change the subject. I'm enjoying getting to know you better."
- "I guess that's only fair, but you may be here a lot longer than you bargained for!"
- "I think I'd enjoy that."
- "Is this making you uncomfortable? We could talk about it another time if you want."
- "I'd be happy to. First, though, I'd just like to mention that I once knew someone with a similar quirk, and it ended up giving her a lot of trouble she wouldn't let other people see. After a while it got out of hand and could really have hurt her. Luckily, a friend helped her figure out what was going on. It was starting to take over her life and it was really scary for her. It turned out to be a chemical imbalance that could be treated, and she got her life back. Anyway, I was concerned that maybe this was beginning to happen to you and I wanted to help if I could because, you see, one of the things I learned was that the sooner one starts treatment with this thing the less of one's life gets consumed and the sooner one gets it back. It was kind of presumptuous of me to butt in like that, but I didn't want to leave you to suffer needlessly just because I was scared to say anything. I'm really sorry."

"I THINK IT'S TIME TO TALK ABOUT YOU. I COULD GO ON ALL NIGHT ABOUT CHANGES IN YOUR BEHAVIOR AND WHAT THEY MIGHT MEAN. ARE YOU GAME?"

- "I guess I did a good job of setting myself up for that! Okay, do your worst."
- "How do you know that wasn't my plan all along?"
- "You're a good sport. I hope you realize my intentions were good. Actually, it was really hard for me to bring up the subject."
- "As long as the subject isn't closed forever."

"WHY WON'T THIS GO AWAY?"

- "It's really getting to you, isn't it?"
- "I wish I knew."
- "I've been worried about you; I just hate to see you suffer like this. So I hope you don't mind, but I've been doing a little research. It seems there are all kinds of things that could be causing this, and a doctor could figure out which one it is in your case."
- "You think it's getting worse, don't you? That must be so frightening."
- "I've been doing some research, and one of the possibilities is that it could be a form of anxiety. You've been under so much stress for so long that it doesn't seem as far-fetched as you might think. It turns out it's extremely common—one in eight adults have some form of this at any given time. And I was relieved to find that there are good treatments. Anyway, it doesn't usually go away by itself, and doctors usually rule out other things before they consider this. But it

might be worth having someone do some tests because it could be some simple thing that can easily be corrected."

"I CAN'T."

- "I know. It's okay." (Don't say, "Yes, you can." It trivializes it.)
- "It's okay. We can try another time. Any number of times. Whenever you feel like trying, let me know."

Part III

॰ঽ৹

ACTIONS MATTER
What to Do

"A look is often the very soul of what one says."

~ HELEN KELLER

Chapter Eleven

Beyond Words

ॐ

What Body Language Can Do

*T*he focus of this book is on words, but words don't operate in a vacuum. They can be cold or warm, sarcastic or comforting, accusing or praising, belittling or healing. And it is the way we deliver them that makes the difference.

The same words can be spoken in a multitude of ways. The way you use your voice, the expression on your face, the way you hold your body, how much space there is between you and the other person, even the way you move or gesture can affect the way your words are heard.

If you were speaking a foreign language, all these things would convey much of what you intend. Even if none of your words could be understood, most of the underlying message would be. Little would be lost.

We have all had experiences similar to this. Perhaps sitting in a restaurant and noticing the people a few tables away. We can't make out the words, but we hear the voices and see the interaction. We know whether the conversation is friendly or not; whether the people have a working relationship or a social one; whether they are courting or have been together a long time; whether the conversation is a balanced discussion, or one person is questioning the other, or one person is raking the other over the coals. We can feel if there is happiness or sadness or anger or confusion or simple pleasantness. And all without words.

So once we think about the words we want to say, we need to give the same consideration to how we say them. We tend to do this unconsciously—both when we speak and when we interpret what we are hearing. This chapter will help you become aware of the various components so your words can be as supportive as possible. Here are elements of body language you might want to keep in mind.

THE WAY YOU USE YOUR VOICE

- Tone of voice (cold/warm, sharp/gentle, sarcastic/enthusiastic, interested/dismissive)
- Volume (loud, normal range, soft)
- Pitch (high, normal range, low)
- Speed
- Pauses

YOUR FACIAL EXPRESSION

- Stiff or expressive
- Smiling, frowning, interested, confused, frustrated, angry, sad, bored, neutral, caring
- Making eye contact or avoiding it
- Open or closed
- Objective or subjective (not taking sides or giving away your opinion versus appearing negative or positive, showing your opinion, being judgmental)

HOW YOU HOLD YOUR BODY

- Tense or relaxed
- Leaning toward or away
- Welcoming or pushing away

HOW MUCH SPACE YOU LEAVE BETWEEN YOU

- Giving space
- Keeping distance
- Invading space

THE WAY YOU MOVE OR GESTURE

- Fluid or jerky
- Expansive or held in

People will read these physical messages based on their knowledge of you and their experience with people in general. The better they know you, the more they will pick up from these kinds of cues. The person you care about will be sensitive to anything that differs from the usual and is likely to focus on that. His interpretation of the differences could be positive or negative—just as your response could be more or less supportive. Often, that interpretation could be on an unconscious level, which makes the effect more powerful.

We associate these cues with people's emotions, opinions, judgments of us, and degree of caring. They may mean different things to different people at different times, and some are culturally based. When someone speaks loudly, we may think he is angry or impatient or thinks us incapable of understanding. When someone speaks slowly, we may think she is taking her time, thinking things through, looking for the right words, or we may interpret it similarly to someone speaking loudly. When people keep a physical space between them and us, we might see it as a mark of respect or we might see it as a symbol of emotional distancing. On the other hand, when someone leans towards us or scoots a chair closer, we could see it as an invasion of space and privacy or as a way of telling us he'd like to be closer emotionally and is open to listening and providing support.

The important thing is to be aware that we send nonverbal messages and that people receive them. Be prepared to check if they are coming through the right way. If people don't react in the way you expect or hope, let them know how you'd hoped they would have interpreted them.

"*To touch with the thought is almost the same as to touch with the hand.*"

— VICTOR HUGO

Chapter Twelve

Beyond Language

୬

THE POWER OF SILENCE

*W*ords aren't the only way we communicate. Silence can also be very powerful.

We usually think of silence as a withdrawal, a refusal, or a distancing. Something negative, hurtful, and uncaring. But silence can be loving, comforting, accepting, and healing. Many of our most intimate moments, when we feel closest to others, are forged in silence and nurtured by it.

As babies, we have all been held and rocked in silence, and many of us have felt the same peace and strength and tenderness as we held babies ourselves. Sitting in silence, hugging, and walking hand in hand are often the times when we feel closest to the people we love. Words are an imperfect bridge between people. The communion of silence and touch is more direct and less liable to misinterpretation.

The language of comfort is often rooted in silence. We don't need words to communicate warmth, our presence, our caring, our reaching out, our wanting to be there for the person we care about. And sometimes silence conveys that best.

Let this chapter remind you of the things we can sense without words, and that we can communicate in this way with others. When we share silence together, we feel the sharing of breath and air; we have the sense of being together in the same moment without effort to do anything or convey any kind of content; we just feel the relaxation of being with the other.

This is so important because one of the things we realize as we grow up is how essentially alone we are inside our own skins. And we feel most alone when we are grieving, in pain, or afraid. Yet it is precisely at these times that we most need to feel as one with another human being.

When we feel most alone, it is in silence that we can approach one another—just the simple patient being together, in parallel, sharing time and space and air. And in those moments, loneliness and terror can be briefly supplanted by something stronger.

Words help. But it is silence that can make barriers seem to fall away, reduce the sense of separateness we all have, and create the feeling that the deepest essence of each of us is touching.

We have all been the recipients of this at times when it made all the difference. We can create this feeling, too. Even when it can't be healing, it is nourishing, and at least provides an oasis of peace.

It is not necessary to be in a romantic relationship, or a family relationship, or a close friendship to tap into this. People do this all the time in a simple exchange of glances, or in sharing a ride somewhere in a comfortable and companionable silence, in working together on hands-on projects or even processing paperwork, and when sharing a physical activity.

"*We must not let the walls close in.*"

꩜ ELEANOR ROOSEVELT

Chapter Thirteen

Triggers and Flashpoints

ॐ

Making Their World Safe

In the case of ordinary nerves and anxiousness, facing fears often helps to resolve them or at least to increase one's confidence when facing them again in the future. Anxiety disorders are not an ordinary case of nerves, though, and behaving as if they are can make them worse. So it's not a good idea to insist that someone do something he's anxious about or push someone to face what she fears.

In some forms of anxiety, such as in the case of a phobia, gradual exposure can make a difference and help a person learn to overcome a fear and live more fully. But this needs to be done very carefully and in treatment, and a professional with experience is more likely to do this successfully. Your focus should be on encouragement, not on forcing someone to do something.

Unless they are well on their way to recovery, the anxiety is under control, or they are under the guidance of a professional when putting themselves in situations that cause anxiety, they could end up with a panic attack and even put themselves in danger. The experience could also deepen the anxiety.

The best help you can give is to encourage professional help and leave treatment to the professionals. In the meantime, you can help the people you care about work around their anxiety so that they can build strength and confidence in conducting the other parts of their lives.

This means respecting the sources and triggers of their anxiety and helping the people you care about avoid them. We all need to feel safe before we can take risks, secure before we can venture out even in a small way. You can help them build that safety; this chapter focuses on how you can do that.

AVOIDING PANIC ATTACKS

FIND OUT WHAT THEIR TRIGGERS ARE

With some things, such as a specific phobia to snakes, it might seem obvious that you would avoid the reptile exhibit at the zoo. But for some people, the phobia might extend to pictures of snakes or scenes in movies that contain snakes. So it's always better to ask than to assume. If someone you care about has shared the fact that he has an anxiety disorder, thank him for trusting you, tell him how sorry you are he has to deal with this, and offer to help. Here are some things you could say regarding triggers:

- "I'm glad you told me, because I'd never want to contribute to this flaring up in any way, even inadvertently. Could we sit down sometime so you can tell me what sorts of things trigger this so I can help you avoid them?"
- "I don't know a lot about what you are going through. Do you think we could talk about it sometime so I don't become part of the problem?"
- "Thank you for telling me. I hope there are ways I can help you and that you'll tell me what they are, even if that's just things I shouldn't do."

Help them draw boundaries

When a person suffering from anxiety tells you his triggers, they may appear at first to be a number of unrelated, isolated things. On the other hand, they may suggest patterns, which will make it easier for you to draw boundaries. These patterns can come in various forms. For example, the triggers may have something geographical in common, or something topographical (near water, near rock formations, at certain elevations). They may relate to the size of a space (very large or very small), the size of a gathering or to certain characteristics of people (such as highly educated). They could relate to conversational topics or a body type, or to certain numbers or colors. Search for common ground.

When you have found one or more patterns to the triggers, you will be able to predict when a given situation, upcoming event, or proposed outing is likely to contain those triggers. This will help you steer clear of them, or at least prepare him for the trigger in advance. It will make it possible for you to discuss the likelihood of a trigger occurring and give him the chance to make an informed decision about going. It may even open up his thinking about possible coping strategies.

Protect their dignity

Though she may have trusted you with the fact that she is struggling with anxiety and been willing to discuss the triggers she has identified, this doesn't mean she'll want to share any of this with other people. She will probably want to protect her privacy and maintain her dignity. You can help her do that by running interference for her.

Try to pay attention. If an activity is suggested that would include her, and you realize that it will involve one of her triggers, volunteer that you yourself aren't particularly interested in it. If she is there when it is suggested and says she isn't keen on it, say you feel the same way or suggest something else to do. Depending on whether the trigger arises out of the activity itself or something about the details surrounding it, you could suggest a different activity, a better location, a different time of day, or even that the group split up and go in different directions.

What you want to do is make the backing out seem natural, infrequent, and not appear to be coming only from her. This is important, because these situations can come up frequently and she could start to feel uncomfortable, embarrassed, and resented if other people begin to see her as difficult, negative, or not wanting to spend time with them.

When you keep it natural and low-key, it will not look as if you are interceding. It will look as if you just happen to feel the same way, and she will feel supported.

GET SOME GUIDANCE

If the person you care about has been evaluated, then he may have been diagnosed with a specific form of anxiety. If he is willing to share that with you, you will be able to learn more about that disorder and provide help in more targeted ways. If he is comfortable about your talking with the professional he trusts, you could get some guidance that would help both of you. (See chapter 2 for more on working with professionals.)

This can be important because what may be generally true for many triggers may not be true for all of them. So knowing how to provide support and validation without causing someone to isolate himself even further would be something a professional could help with.

It's also important to keep in mind that any kind of therapy will have a better chance of success if everyone is working from the same page. If the things you are saying run counter to what a therapist is saying, the person who is already struggling with anxiety now has to struggle with mixed messages. If the therapist is working on changes in thinking or behavior in one way and you are coming at it in another way, the person you care about may feel conflicted or have to use up energy fighting one or both of you—energy better used to fight the anxiety itself. As in many things in life, a coordinated approach is best.

If you know the person you care about is seeing someone, even if your relationship doesn't lend itself to talking to the therapist, or to even bringing up the possibility, it might be possible to suggest that some additional knowledge could make a difference.

Things you could say:

- "I don't know if you'd feel comfortable telling me anything about the plan you and your therapist have put together, but if there's something that the people around you should do differently, I'd be happy to try."
- "If there's something in particular that you are working on, and there's a way I can help, please tell me."
- "I know this is hard and that you are working at it. I don't want to get in the way of what you are trying to do. If I am, please tell me what I should change."
- "I feel honored that you told me what's going on and that you are getting professional advice. What's really hard for me is not knowing how to help and being worried that I might be doing something that makes this even harder for you. I guess what I'm trying to say is that I feel I'm flying blind. If there is a way for me to know more about what you are going through or what I could be doing to help, point me there!"

BE REALISTIC

We teach our children to be strong and self-reliant and to face new situations without fear, but we also teach them to be cautious and to be afraid of those things that will endanger them: a hot stove, the edge of a cliff, walking on railroad tracks, crossing the road without looking. We teach them to be alert, to pay attention, to think things through, to weigh actions and their consequences. Though we hate to make children afraid of anything, we do this deliberately and with reason. In the times of greatest danger, it is our fear that protects us.

But this can boomerang on those who suffer from anxiety. Their very fear can endanger them. It can paralyze them in the moment of greatest danger. It can isolate them from those who could help. It can cause them to flee into the fear. As an extreme example, someone afraid of heights who freezes or panics at the edge of a cliff is more likely to have what she most fears happen—falling to her death—than someone who is relaxed.

Panic is not only terrifying because of the danger it poses to the person you care about, it is terrifying to experience. It is a feeling as overwhelming in its intensity as the deepest love, as paralyzing as the darkest pain that takes one's breath at the loss of a child.

DEALING WITH PANIC ATTACKS

WHEN PANIC HAPPENS

It is not always possible to avoid a situation that will trigger anxiety or a panic attack. Fortunately, recognizing that someone is in such a situation can help to minimize the effects. It would be wonderful if we could see when panic is approaching (because it can engulf someone in seconds), to know what to do to head it off, and to know how to act if she has been seized by it. Sometimes we can, sometimes we can't. However, there are some cues and some tools that can help us cope when panic descends.

WHAT TO LOOK FOR

What sort of things tend to happen at the beginning of an anxiety attack or just before it starts to take hold? Are there things he does? Are there things she says? Is there something different about their appearance, their body language, their behavior? You may not be able to head it off, yet recognizing the warning signs might help you help him through it. Once it is starting to happen he may not be able to tell you, so it's a good idea to talk about this ahead of time so you will know what to look for. If a person has shared his concerns, ask him to share his insights, too.

The warning signs may not be the same for everyone, yet some things are common to a lot of people and that can be a starting place:

- Starts to walk more slowly.
- Sudden stops and starts.
- Stops talking suddenly.
- Pitch of voice gets higher.
- Voice drops to a whisper.
- Doesn't seem to hear what you are saying or doesn't answer.
- Facial expression freezes.
- No expression on face at all (as if wiped clean).
- Body tenses up.
- Hands clench, form fists, are clasped together, or thrust into pockets.
- Stays back and won't approach what the rest of the group is heading towards.
- Gets very fidgety.

- Folds arms across chest, holds self in some way.
- Bites lip, digs fingernails into self.
- Looks forward, then back, then forward, then back, as if trying to decide whether or not to turn around.
- Becomes very pale, very red, or looks green.
- Suddenly starts sweating profusely.
- Pulse rate accelerates; blood pressure soars.

How to head it off

The earlier in the process you notice that something is wrong, the easier it is to head it off. The best course, if possible, is to create an immediate change in the situation—such as removing the trigger or removing her from the situation.

You might say:

- "I'm ready to go. Let's head out."
- "This isn't for me after all. Let's head back."
- "Bill and I are going to take a break. See you all later."
- "I'm not big on mosquitoes. We'll leave you to the lake—Tanisha and I are going to camp out at the Holiday Inn! See you in the morning."
- "We're not in the mood to scramble over the rocks. We're going to check out the wildflowers, instead."
- "This party is too rambunctious for me. We're going to go someplace quiet and talk."
- "We're not on any sort of timetable here. You go on ahead. We'll catch up later."
- "How about a time out? Let's take a walk and talk this through."
- "It's okay to be nervous. Let's visualize how it's going to go."

- "Let's duck out for a minute and release a little tension. We could do some breathing and some isometrics."
- "You still have a few minutes before you have to go up there and give your speech. Look over the audience from here; pick someone out right now; make eye contact; try nodding to him or waving."
- "Tell me your first sentence." (Pause.) "I like that. It really makes me want to hear more."
- "Why did you pick this topic?" (Pause.) "It sounds important. It sounds as if it will make a difference to your audience. That's great."
- "These things make me nervous. I need to talk to someone or have something in my hands."
- "It's pretty close in here. Would you mind walking over to the window to get some air?"
- "I don't know too many people here, do you?"

WHEN PANIC HITS

Talking to people when they are in the midst of a panic attack is tough because they will be in the grip of something they can't control and they may not be able to process what you say to them. They could be shaking, gasping, struggling for breath, unable to get words out, screaming, crying, frozen in place and unable to reason.

This is scary to see even if it is someone you don't know. If it is someone you care about, you can feel overwhelmed, too. It's important not to panic yourself and to keep your tone of voice and your body language calm. Don't touch him unless he gives you permission first, or until you can gauge his reaction when you tell him you are going to put an arm around him.

Panic attacks can look like heart attacks, so if you've never seen this happen to him before, ask him if this is something new. If he says that it is, it would be a good idea to check things out medically. You might say:

- "Do you need to go to the emergency room?"
- "Would you like me to get you to an emergency room or would you rather call an ambulance?"

However, if this has happened before, and he has seen a doctor who determined that this was a panic attack, you can help him ride it through. Ironically, when anxiety causes a panic attack, the fear of the panic attack itself only creates a lot more anxiety. And panic attacks don't only look like heart attacks, they can also feel like heart attacks. This means that people need to be reminded that this is probably not a heart attack and that it will pass.

You can help them calm down by being confident, talking quietly, and providing reassurance. The aim is to slow down their body rhythms so that the heart slows, the pulse evens out, and all their rhythms become regular. It may help for you to know that anxiety attacks tend to last about ten to thirty minutes and that what people need most is the conviction of those around them that they will be safe.

SOME THINGS YOU CAN SAY:

- "I'm here. I'll wait with you until this passes."
- "I'm going to put an arm around you, if that's okay."
- "Let's try walking to a spot where you'll be more comfortable."
- "I think this might be anxiety. It's going to be okay."
- "It feels a little cold in here. How about a sweater or blanket? Or I could put an arm around you to help you get warm."

- "Do you want to go outside and get a little air?"
- "I want to help you catch your breath. Let's try breathing together, all right? Try watching me. Or listen to me. Breathe in." [Hold a couple of seconds.] "Breathe out. Again. Breathe in. Breathe out."
- "You're swallowing so much air. Let's try slowing your breathing down. Breathe with me. Count. On three, breathe in. On three, breathe out. Okay, here we go. One, two, three, breathe."
- "If it's okay with you, I'm going to rub your shoulders. Maybe that will help. Okay?"
- "Let's walk over there and sit down together. You'll be okay. We'll just give this a few minutes."
- "You are not dying."
- "If you want a ride to the doctor, just tell me."

SOME THINGS YOU CAN DO:

- Ask them if they have any medication they are supposed to take when this happens. Then help them find it and take it.
- Ask them what they need and then make it happen.
- Offer a glass of warm milk.
- Stay with them.
- Focus their attention on something other than their symptoms—small talk, or some simple activity.
- Put on some calming music or something you know is a favorite.
- Have her brush her teeth, wash her face, or brush her hair; offer to brush her hair for her. (Sometimes a routine activity can create a sense of calm because of its familiarity and association with self-care.)

WHAT IF HE IS HYPERVENTILATING?

Sometimes a person in the midst of a panic attack will start to hyperventilate. In that case, taking deep breaths might intensify what is happening.

What does hyperventilating look like? It's a combination of deep and rapid breathing; it can sound raspy and look as if someone is gasping for breath, or breathing in huge gulps but not getting enough. In the process, he will be pushing out much more carbon dioxide than usual, which can make him feel dizzy or faint.

The key to restoring balance is to get some of that carbon dioxide back into the system quickly. An easy way to do that is to help him breathe into a paper bag. If he holds it around his mouth and exhales into it without removing the bag, he can then breathe back in all that carbon dioxide. Many people don't realize that low carbon dioxide levels decrease blood circulation. Increasing blood circulation has the benefit of getting more oxygen to the brain. In a roundabout way, breathing into a paper bag doesn't just interrupt the hyperventilating: it feeds the brain.

"Gardening is an instrument of grace."

～ MAY SARTON

Chapter Fourteen

Sources of Strength

୬

Other Ways to Give

When people we care about suffer from anxiety, we notice how tense and overwrought they are, how drained of energy, and how they increasingly think of themselves as weak. We want to ease the anxiety and help them restore some calm to their lives, to slow the energy drain and try to replenish their strength, to renew their faith in themselves. This chapter suggests things we can say and things we can do to give them the strength to go on.

We need to remind them that there is more to them than this fear, that there is more in their lives than this fear, and that there is a life awaiting them both now and once they've reached the other side.

The support you give them through words and actions is important. When you give them words, you help them focus on a new way of seeing themselves. When you help them act, you take them out of themselves so that their attention is on something other than their anxiety.

This is not easy to do. People suffering from anxiety will resist what you say and what you encourage them to do. Be careful to say only what you believe is true and to accept when people don't want to follow your suggestions. Just try again another time.

THINGS YOU CAN DO:

- Help her make a list of accomplishments.
- Help him make a list of his character traits.
- Help her list her friends.
- Help him list things he's done to support other people.
- Help her remember something else she has tackled and overcome.
- Tell him why you love him. Be specific.
- Ask her why she loves you. Ask her to be specific.
- Help him remember the things he loves to do (because he may not be able to).
- Write these lists down so they can look at them whenever they need shoring up.

THINGS THAT CALM:

Water: Unless someone is hydrophobic, water is soothing and calming.
- Suggest a shower.
- Offer to shampoo his hair.
- Go swimming.
- Soak her feet.
- Throw pebbles in a pond.
- Watch waves.
- Listen to a tape of waves crashing the shore.
- Watch boats sail along a lake.
- Hold a shell to the ear.

Warmth: Even if fire is part of his anxiety, other forms of warmth are comforting.

- Heating pads.
- Hot water bottle.
- Electric blanket.
- Cuddling and bundling.
- Warm food.
- Sitting by the fire (if appropriate).

Comfort foods: Some foods seem to nourish our souls, particularly the favorite foods of childhood and what Mom served when we were sick.

- Soup.
- Cereal.
- Mashed potatoes.
- Custards and puddings.
- Stew.
- Pot pies.
- Tea with honey.
- Ice cream.
- Jell-O.
- Hot chocolate (not too much because caffeine can rev one up).

Touch: Some people flinch from touch, but most feel reassured when skin meets skin. Touch can be an affirmation of life.

- Try laying a hand on his shoulder.
- Offer to rub her neck.
- Suggest a massage.
- Stroke his hair.
- Lay your hand on her cheek.
- Wrap him in a blanket or scarf.
- Give her a sweater of yours to wear.
- Offer soft pillows and stuffed animals to hold.

Aromas: Smells can help people relax, particularly smells that remind us of good food, good times, and people we love.

- Put a spice in a pot of water and let it simmer for a while— cinnamon, nutmeg, vanilla, chocolate, or any other food smell the person you care about loves.
- Give him some aromatic candles.
- Get some potpourri with a scent she likes, or create your own.
- Try scenting a pillow with a soothing smell such as lavender.
- Infuse the air with citrus smells—orange, in particular, can be uplifting.

Breathing: Focusing on breathing can take the edge off.
- Count out slow breaths.
- Introduce yoga.
- Remind her of the breathing taught for labor (but be careful not to focus on panting because that can lead to hyperventilating when someone is on the verge of a panic attack).

Activity: Focusing on something else for a while can also help them feel a small measure of control.
- Exercise that engages the body.
- An activity that engages the mind, such as reading or playing chess.
- A mindless, repetitive activity, such as folding laundry, shelling peas, shucking corn, digging dirt, chopping wood, washing windows, waxing a car, kneading bread, weeding, picking apples or berries.
- Rowing a boat.
- Taking a walk.
- Punching a bag.
- Crunching numbers.
- Jogging or running.

Routine: Unless someone is suffering from OCD, it's a good idea to encourage the person you care about to structure his days.

- Eating meals at regular times.
- Going to bed and getting up at the same time each day.
- Setting up regular appointments for exercise, therapy, meetings with friends—the same time each week.
- Establishing the same work schedule for each day.

We all tend to depend on routine to counteract feelings of fear or the loss of safety and security. This is a way we calm ourselves. Routine and predictability help to ward off stress because they are comfortable and familiar and give one the sense of being in control.

THINGS THAT RENEW

Nurturing life
- Doing something for someone else.
- Gardening.
- Tending to house plants.
- Caring for a pet.
- Connecting to other people—with a smile, a word, a touch, a nod.
- Spending time with children.

Creating something
- Drawing, painting, sculpting, photography.
- Writing letters, stories, essays, poems, riddles.
- Knitting, crocheting, quilting, embroidery, needlepoint, sewing.
- Composing a song or other musical piece.

- Working with crafts.
- Inventing a practical solution to something.
- Cooking.
- Building a model.
- Assembling a jigsaw puzzle.
- Working on a joint project.

Engaging in music
- Playing an instrument.
- Joining with others in song and music-making.
- Attending a concert.
- Listening to music.
- Arranging a song.
- Dancing.

Bringing order out of chaos
- Organizing paperwork.
- Catching up on files.
- Catching up on mail.
- Cleaning out a drawer or closet.
- Making a doable list for the day and checking things off, one by one.
- Committing to doing three things that week and scheduling them.

Sustaining oneself with work
- One's job.
- An avocation.
- Maintaining a household.
- Anything one carves out as a personal responsibility.

Anything that completely focuses the attention (and is not related to their anxiety)
- Something beautiful in nature.
- A competitive sport or race.
- A problem to solve.
- A hobby.
- A fast-paced film.
- A favorite book or book in a favorite genre (mystery, sci-fi, romance, etc.).

The memory of a relaxing moment
- A walk on the beach.
- Wind blowing through one's hair.
- A rainbow.
- A ride in a convertible.
- Watching clouds.
- A picnic.
- A wonderful hug.
- A special smile.

Laughter (as long as it doesn't focus on anxiety or its source)
- Jokes.
- Memories of funny or silly moments.
- Comedians.
- Humorous movies.
- Bringing laughter to someone else.
- Introducing comedy to children (and seeing it through their eyes).

Nature
- A sunrise or sunset.
- The stars in the sky.

- A flower turning toward the light.
- Rain drizzling on one's face.
- Trees in bud.
- Fall foliage.
- A pool of water.

Beauty, other people's needs, other kinds of thoughts, work, order, a sense of being part of something larger while having some control—all these help. And creating helps most of all. Whether it is creating happiness for someone else, expressing his feelings or venting hers, making order where there wasn't any, transforming notes on a page into music he can hear, or creating something no one has made before, all forms of creating affirm and renew the self. Because when we create, we are giving something life. Nothing can be more positive than that.

Part IV

꙰

LIVING DAY BY DAY

"Feelings, too, are facts."

∽ ELEANOR ROOSEVELT

Chapter Fifteen

Seesawing Emotions

ॐ

How to Respond

When someone you care about is suffering from anxiety, it is likely that you will encounter situations you are unsure how to handle. Even when they look like something you've seen before, you may wonder if you should approach them in the same way. It could be something she is doing, something he is refusing to do, something she says, or an intense emotional response that just seems to hang on. This section tries to prepare you for specific situations that tend to come up. This first chapter lists some of the emotions you are likely to encounter when talking to a person suffering from anxiety, such as anger, guilt, or embarrassment. The following chapter focuses on situations common to people struggling with anxiety disorders. Both chapters suggest ways to help and respond. The key is to take things day by day, to remember that each person is unique, and to meet each situation as it comes with understanding and sensitivity.

EMPATHIZING WITH THEIR EMOTIONS

People suffering from anxiety may react in different ways, but they may be feeling many of the same emotions, and those emotions can end up assailing you, too.

None of these emotions are surprising given the way anxiety can assault people's minds and bodies, but you may need to be prepared for their intensity, their duration, and their resistance to the way you might ordinarily try to bring calm.

ANGER

Anxiety interferes with people's lives. It affects what they can do and when and where they can do it. They realize it affects the people around them, and they're shaken when their usual ways of coping don't work. So people suffering from anxiety will often feel angry at themselves for not being able to make it go away, and angry at the situation for existing in the first place. And when they vent that anger, they may end up getting angry at you.

Don't tell them to calm down. Think about how you feel when you are upset. It can make you angrier if someone tells you to "cool your jets." When you tell someone to calm down, you are trying to help them by easing the tension. They, however, need to vent. Plus, they may hear that you don't think their anger is warranted, or that their expressing it reflects poorly on them. So when you tell them to calm down, you may just steam them up more. This doesn't help them, and it can make you the target of their anger.

It's better to agree with them. Tell them how angry you would be in their shoes. Even that you are angry on their behalf. This will give them some relief and will make them feel you support them.

EMBARRASSMENT AND HUMILIATION

We all want to look as if we have it together. People who suffer from anxiety know they don't, but it adds to their discomfort that other people can see it, too. Under other circumstances, they would know this was temporary and have a way to explain it away. But with anxiety, they're not sure what they are dealing with, don't feel they have control over it, have no idea how long it will last, and are either unwilling or unable to explain it. So it's not surprising they don't want to put themselves in situations that expose their anxiety.

Respect their feelings. Think about how to draw attention away from them. Make sure they know that you aren't embarrassed by their behavior and that you think no less of them. Tell them you think more of them for dealing with this illness with such grace and strength. That you don't know if you could do what they do.

Tell them you understand they may feel embarrassed, but it doesn't change the way you think of them and it shouldn't change the way they think of themselves. There is so much more to them than this.

SHAME, GUILT, AND STIGMA

Shame is not the same as embarrassment or humiliation. Embarrassment and humiliation have to do with being exposed to others and losing their respect. Shame is about how he views himself, about his own self-respect. How can he expect anyone to respect him if he doesn't respect himself? How can he subject them to spending time with him? Why would they want to be his friends? So he will do his best to push those friends away before they see this "truth" about him, before they go away on their own. And he will use any means to accomplish that—

withdrawal, anger, rudeness, forgetfulness, lack of availability, pretending he doesn't care.

Then this will make him feel guilty, not just for letting himself down but for letting down everyone else: for hurting his friends without explaining why, for not living up to promises to family, for not being able to carry out his job the way he'd like to.

This is where friends can help. If you see the changes and think there may be a diagnosable condition that is contributing to this, and if it seems that this is not something he has considered, it might help to raise the possibility. As discussed in chapter 5, sometimes putting a label on an illness—helping someone see that his behavior may be due to an illness—can help take away the shame. If this is an illness, he is not at fault for having it, and he can seek treatment.

FEAR

All of us, in order to have self-respect and feel independent, depend on four additional basic things. These are: a feeling of control, a sense of purpose, a sense of who we are, and a connection with other people. These give our lives meaning and make us feel we have some autonomy in the world.

The loss of any one of these can hurt, and the loss of two can really shake us. Anxiety threatens all of these, and that can generate terrible fear. It wouldn't be normal if it didn't!

It's logical and rational to be afraid under these circumstances. So, as discussed in chapter 7, it's not helpful to tell the person you care about not to be afraid. Instead, acknowledge the fear and follow up with the reassurance of your support. You might say, "This is really scary, isn't it, but we'll get through this as we've gotten through other things."

SHIVERING AND SHAKING

This is a physical expression of fear. Don't let it scare you. Just be there for her while she goes through it. Try talking to her calmly. Maybe hold her hand, or see if she can try sipping a glass of water. If she has trouble breathing or speaking, it could be a panic attack. Try getting her to breathe slowly, to count with her as she inhales and count again as she exhales. Give her time. Once shivering and shaking starts, the body takes over and she can't just throw a mental switch to make it stop.

This kind of reaction, which can also include chills and perspiration, can happen as easily when someone is anticipating an anxiety-producing situation as it can when in an anxiety-producing situation. This means it can happen before an event, during an event, or when remembering an event. Regardless of when it happens, it is no less real, no less frightening, and no less debilitating.

SCREAMING AND CRYING

This is a way of expressing anger and fear. Or of expressing grief for the losses they are facing, because as time goes on they may think they'll never get those things back. Most people would need to react this way when faced with so much. Let them do it; don't ask them to stop.

Realize that on the inside, they might feel like doing it all the time, yet they don't. After letting them know that you feel their reaction is human and natural, let them know how courageous they must be not to be screaming and crying all the time, and how much willpower they must have. Let them know that you don't know if you could do what they do.

SHRINKING INTO THEMSELVES

Some people suffering from anxiety seem to collapse inside themselves; others may keep a stiff facade but isolate themselves from people and situations they used to welcome. Both are a form of shrinking away that can be a reaction to fear or embarrassment. They think that if they avoid certain situations, maybe their anxiety will lessen. And that if it happens anyway, at least other people won't see it. Unfortunately, neither of these is necessarily true. The anxiety may not happen when and where they think it will, and it may happen just where they thought it would be safe. Isolating themselves from the support of friends will not help to control their anxiety, and it may in fact make their friends realize that something is wrong.

Shrinking into oneself could also indicate the beginning stages of depression. So if you are concerned about someone, and you think he might be suffering from depression or anxiety or both, and as far as you know he isn't getting any treatment, you might want to suggest a checkup. (Chapter 1 reviews key symptoms of anxiety and depression.)

HOW THIS AFFECTS YOU

When you are around someone who is angry, afraid, or upset, you can end up feeling these emotions yourself, particularly at those times when your efforts don't seem to be making a difference. If you are prepared for this, they will be easier to deal with. What helps most is accepting that what you do will not work all the time, or right away, or always in a way you can see.

Sometimes absolutely nothing you say or do will work. Other times, they will make a difference you can measure. Or perhaps a particular approach may work one time but not another time.

You need to consider that what appears to be no change could actually be the stop of a slide; in other words, if you hadn't been there, it might have gotten worse.

The important thing is to be flexible, to have a number of tools in your tool kit, and to hang in there. Over the long haul, what you say and do does make a difference.

RESPONDING TO RESISTANCE

When you come into contact with these emotions, you might feel bombarded, and you are likely to meet with some level of resistance from the person who is suffering. It can help to recognize that the person suffering from anxiety may have built a tight wall around herself. As isolating as you see it, she sees it as a comfort zone, and she doesn't want to risk stepping outside of it.

When you try to talk to her about what is happening, to get him to do something with you along the lines of the activities discussed in chapter 14, "Sources of Strength," or to encourage her to have a doctor check her health, it can be difficult to know what to do with the resistance. Here are some general suggestions on what you can say as the resistance continues. (The next chapter will include specific suggestions for different kinds of resistance situations.)

KEEPING THE DOOR OPEN

- "Maybe another time."
- "How about we try that next week?"
- "I've got an unexpected block of time tomorrow. How about we do something together then?"

- "I hope we can do it sometime. It might be fun. It would give us a chance to spend time together, and maybe it would get me out of my own rut."
- "I care about you. When you feel like talking, I'll feel like listening. Okay?"
- "I look forward to when we can go there/do that/talk about this."

REINTRODUCING THE SUBJECT

- "I thought I'd see if we could make plans for tomorrow? Can you get free?"
- "I'd still like to try that activity we were talking about last week. Could we set up a time?"
- "I miss you and would love to get together. I know you're really busy (or feeling drained or stressed), but please give it a try. It might do us both good."
- "I'm hoping things have eased up a little for you and we could compare calendars."
- "I'd really like to talk. When would be a good time?"
- "You can ask me anything, you know, and I will do my best to answer or find an answer."
- "I hope you'll tell me if there's something I can help with. I'd like to help and, if it's something I can do, I will do it. If not, I'll find someone who can."
- "I really enjoyed that trip we made a few months ago. Let's plan something else."

CHOOSING THE RIGHT TIME TO APPROACH

There is no perfect time to approach someone. The best thing to do is to use your life experience, your common sense, and your intuition. Sometimes you can feel when someone is open to a suggestion or has barricaded himself behind walls. Sometimes you can sense that not enough time has passed since the last time you brought it up or made a suggestion. It won't help for him to feel harassed so that he changes his view of you from encouraging friend to insistent pest.

That being said, it's better to make a suggestion when someone is relaxed. She'll be more receptive and less defensive then. And rather than introducing the topic abruptly, it's better to lead up to it after you've already been discussing other things.

Watch for cues so you don't push at the wrong moment. Does he turn away? Does she frown? Does his voice lose animation or energy? Does her smile freeze? Does his body tense up? Does she shift the subject? Does he hedge—say "I don't think so" or "This is not a good time for me"—or put off giving you a definite answer?

DECIDING TO CONFRONT THE ISSUE

When you encounter resistance, it's hard to know what to do. At first, it might make sense to back off for a while, but how do you know when it's time to force a discussion? Your decision will be based on the nature of your relationship, the seriousness of what you see going on, the amount of time that's gone by. The closer your relationship, the more natural it will seem for you to insist on talking about what is happening and for him to accept your doing it. If you have tried bringing up the subject a few times and been pushed away, if some weeks have gone by, if he seems to be functioning less, if she seems to be withdrawing more, if the downhill trend seems to be accelerating, and if you are starting to see effects on someone's overall health, too—changes in weight, sleeping patterns, alertness, energy, appetite, plus some new persistent aches—then it's time to push a little. Time to stop taking no for an answer.

You might say:

- "I know you don't want to talk about this, but I need to tell you what I'm seeing."
- "I need to talk to you. You don't have to answer me, but I really need you to listen."
- "I've been standing by for weeks watching you struggle with something you haven't wanted to talk about. That's okay. You don't have to tell me what it is. What's not okay is what it is doing to you. It's really hurting you. And it seems to be getting worse rather than better. Please get some help with whatever it is, even with figuring out what it is. And if I can help with any of that, I'm ready."
- "Something is going on, and it is taking a toll on you. Whatever it is doesn't seem to be going away. What do you need to be able to deal with it? How can I help you get those things?"
- "Whatever has been happening, it seems to be something one can't go alone. I see it getting harder rather than easier, worse instead of better. You wouldn't let me keep sliding, and I won't stand by and sit on my hands, either. Tell me what you've done so far."
- "I know you value your privacy and I respect that, but your health is more important. Your happiness is more important. I care about what is happening to you, and I want to help. Things can't go on like this; it's time to do something about it."
- "When things keep getting harder, it could be a sign you need outside help. Have you considered getting a medical workup? That a medical condition could be responsible and that there could be a simple treatment for it?"

- "Something is going on that's dragging you down. I'd like to help. If you don't feel you can talk to me about it, maybe I could help by hooking you up with someone you *would* be comfortable with."
- "I've been concerned about you these past few weeks. I know you are a private person so I've held off saying anything, but whatever is bothering you is getting worse. Have you talked to anyone about it? Please don't let it fester; it might only get worse."

DON'T ASSUME THIS HAS NEVER HAPPENED BEFORE. ASK.

- "I've noticed you're tense a lot of the time, and you are having some difficulties doing xyz. Has this happened before?"
- "When this happened before, how did you handle it? How did the people in your life help you? I'd like to help if you'll tell me how."
- "If you've gone through anything like this before, you know it's good to interrupt what's happening so it doesn't get any worse. What have you done so far to rein it in?"
- "If this has never happened before, I want you to know it's like a lot of other things in life—it goes away faster and is easier to handle if you tackle it right away. The longer you wait, the harder it gets."

IF YOU KNOW IT HAS HAPPENED BEFORE BECAUSE YOU WERE THERE AT THE TIME, REMIND HER:

- "It may be hard for you to see because you are so close to it, but the same things are happening now that happened two years ago." [List them.] "We didn't know what we were dealing with then and put off doing anything about it for a long time. And it was so hard for you. Let's lick this early while it's easier to do."

- "You're worrying the way you did before you developed anxiety. Remember the therapist saying that a lot of worrying could trigger anxiety again? Please don't slough it off; do something about it now so you won't have to go through all that again. Think about it."

"Pain is diverse as man. One suffers as one can."

☍ Victor Hugo

Chapter Sixteen

Situation by Situation

ᗡ

One Thing at a Time

*W*hen someone has a physical injury, we expect that activity will be restricted. That she will need help. We remind him, even nag him, to give himself a chance to heal. We explain that we don't want her to aggravate it. We insist that he do less. We implore her to accept help. If someone is hurt mentally, should we do the same?

We don't tend to feel as sure of ourselves when someone we care about is suffering from something that isn't clearly visible in a physical sense. When someone has a broken leg, we can relate sufficiently to anticipate some of the things that would be difficult or impossible to do and we would react accordingly. There are a number of things, however, that you might not anticipate— maybe not even recognize as being part of anxiety—when someone you know is dealing with anxiety. This chapter can't prepare you for everything, but it discusses a variety of situations that you might encounter when someone you care about is struggling with anxiety so that you can understand what you are seeing and become more comfortable about how to respond. In many cases, a situation might give you the opening to talk about what is really happening. And then you might be able to suggest looking into the kinds of help that are available.

I THINK SHE'S ISOLATING HERSELF. WHAT SHOULD I DO?

Talk to her about it. Tell her it seems you haven't been able to get together for a while and that you want to turn that around. Mention that when you've talked on the phone, you've gotten the impression that she doesn't seem to get around much anymore. Ask her if work has been piling up, if she's been feeling okay, if something else is going on that's making demands on her time or is making her want to burrow in a cave for a while.

See if she is relaxed about talking to you about this, or even relieved; that will open the door for more probing. Maybe she'll accept some help from you or even discuss the possibility of help. Maybe she'll be willing to tell you what she needs right now.

If she resists the conversation, just tell her how much you care and move on to another topic. But start calling more often just to say hi, keep the connection going, and help her feel the door is open. (Eventually you may have to confront her more directly.)

I THINK SHE'S HIDING SOMETHING. WHAT CAN I SAY?

Tell her something seems different and it feels as if it's *not* something that is making her happy. Ask her if anything has happened to scare her or if something in her life is causing her a lot of stress. Tell her you don't want to intrude, but you do want to help. Tell her there have been times when you had someone to talk to about your problems and it made all the difference, and if you can be that person for her, you'd like to try.

HE DENIES THERE'S A PROBLEM. HOW SHOULD I RESPOND?

He might be denying that there is a problem because he doesn't want to accept it himself, or because he is afraid of what the problem might be, or because he is afraid of being weak or ill. But he may be much more afraid of something else, and that is of being seen differently from then on—not just by himself but by you and other people who will know. He is afraid that if he is seen differently, he will forever more be treated differently—as if the illness is all people see, as if that's what defines him. It isn't only kids who need approval from their peers. In addition, he may dread the combination of pity, distancing, patronizing, or a lessening of respect that might come with a label.

Make sure he knows that you'll hold in confidence whatever he says. That whatever the problem is, you care and will try to help. Encourage him to check out what is wrong so he doesn't have to keep feeling this way.

HE RESENTS MY BRINGING IT UP. HOW SHOULD I HANDLE THAT?

Sometimes it can help to stay away from the subject for a while. Just be available whenever he wants to talk about other things. This will make talking to you feel natural, and will build a level of trust that will make it easier for him to bring up the subject of anxiety, too.

You can let him know that you see he wants you to drop the subject for a while and that you will honor that request. But make sure you add that you are concerned and that you hope he'll bring it up himself if there's any way you can help, even if it is just to listen. And if time passes—days, weeks—and you don't see a change and he doesn't bring it up, you can gently introduce the subject again.

I TRY TO MAKE PLANS WITH HER, BUT SHE ALWAYS TURNS ME DOWN. WHAT DOES THIS MEAN?

It could mean that she is tired of disappointing people by not being ready, or not showing up, or canceling at the last minute, or always being very late. Either she can't commit, or she thinks it would be best if she just didn't make plans anymore. Instead of this being a sign that something is wrong with your friendship, it could mean that she honors it enough not to abuse it and that she doesn't want to risk losing it. You could suggest that it might be fun to just do things on the spur of the moment from now on, to live spontaneously. If you're both available at the last minute, great. If not, you'll just give it a try another time.

HE COMMITS BUT DOESN'T SHOW UP. HOW SHOULD I INTERPRET THAT?

Don't take it personally. Don't jump to conclusions. Just ask him about it. Say you were concerned and you missed him. Ask if he'd rather do things that weren't planned. Maybe do things on his turf rather than have him travel somewhere else.

HE WON'T GO ANYWHERE WITHOUT ME. HOW CAN I HELP?

See if he'll talk about why he thinks this is happening. Reassure him that you love his company, but you feel he is missing out on things if he always has to adjust to your interests and your availability. Maybe he'll be willing to have a network of friends to do things with. Maybe he'll see that the walls of his world are closing in on him and you'll be able to encourage him to see if there's help to stop them from doing that.

I CAN'T GET HER TO LEAVE THE HOUSE, EVEN WHEN I SAY I'LL GO WITH HER. WHAT CAN I DO?

Sit down and discuss what you are seeing. Say that you know other people have had to deal with this and that there are ways to change it. Ask if you can help find out where to go to get the help to do that. Remind her of how much she is missing and of all the people who miss being with her and seeing her enjoy life the way she used to. Assure her that it is possible to reclaim the other parts of her life.

She doesn't seem to understand this could be an illness. What can I say?

Tell her that there are a number of illnesses that can cause irritability, sadness, a stepped-up metabolism, excessive sweating, trouble breathing, sudden anger, a rapid pulse, trembling, and intense emotions. That these illnesses might be caused by the body producing too much of one chemical or too little of another. Or she could be ingesting too much of one vitamin so that the body can't process it or she might have a deficiency of another. Explain that when doctors figure out where the imbalance is, they can adjust the balance through treatment.

Tell her that if this is what might be happening to her, it could be relatively simple to get her life back. And if it turns out that what she is experiencing is due to an anxiety condition, that could be treated, too. Would she hesitate to have her doctor check her hormone levels if she thought her pancreas or thyroid was producing too much or too little? How does she know that one of these isn't the cause of her symptoms? It could well turn out that way, and if not—if the organ in question happens to be the brain—what difference does it make?

If he won't recognize the possibility of this being anxiety, how can I encourage him to get evaluated?

Let him know how common anxiety problems are. That one in eight adults suffer from an anxiety disorder in this country, and many of them unnecessarily because treatment is readily available. Let him know that many people don't recognize that they could be suffering from anxiety, or they think it's just a passing thing so they don't tell a doctor about the symptoms. Let him know that those who do are relieved to know that it has a name, that it can be dealt with, and that doctors take it in stride because there is a lot of it going around.

WHAT IF HE'S NOT GETTING ANY SLEEP? WON'T THIS MAKE THINGS WORSE?

Lack of sleep seldom helps anyone. And, for most of us, lack of sleep makes it more difficult for us to focus, handle stress, process information, or be productive. It tends to make us irritable, more prone to anger, more prone to cry, more prone to startle. People suffering from anxiety are likely to have interrupted sleep because their fears make it difficult to fall asleep and to stay asleep. So they get a double whammy. If nothing else, help him see the value of getting an evaluation on the sleep issue. Encourage him to be open with the doctor about other things that are going on so that the doctor can determine the underlying problem. Sleeping pills won't get at an underlying problem, and not being able to sleep will only make it that much harder to deal with the anxiety.

WHAT IF SHE'S EATING VORACIOUSLY? WHAT IF HE PICKS AT HIS FOOD? HOW DO THESE FIT IN?

People under stress react to food in two ways. They may eat ravenously for comfort or to give their mouths and hands something to do, or they may lose their appetites altogether because their stomachs won't stop churning or their stress has led to a lot of gas in their digestive systems.

People who have dramatic changes in their eating habits, or who suddenly gain or lose a lot of weight without having talked about wanting to do so, often have something significant happening in their lives. It might not be anxiety, but something else may be going on and it could well be a disease process.

If she's eating a lot but not putting on weight, her thyroid could be out of whack, she could be on an intensive exercise program, she could be seriously ill in some way, or she could have bulimia. If it is bulimia, she is facing an illness that can cause extensive damage to her organs over time if she persists in binging and purging. Fortunately, bulimia is also treatable.

HE USES EVERY SPARE MOMENT FOR EXERCISE. I'M SCARED HE'LL STROKE OUT.

Exercise is a distraction and a method of self-discipline that makes one feel in control. It can also generate endorphins that bring relief because they flood the system with a natural high.

Tell him you've noticed he exercises a lot more than he used to. If he is eliminating other things from his life—such as time with friends and family—because there is no longer time for them, tell him you miss him and that other people do, too. Ask him what led him to rev things up to this degree. Ask if he is trying to reduce stress in his life and if there's anything in particular that has become so much more stressful. Ask him if he has considered the possibility that a medical problem might be causing the stress. And ask him if he had a checkup to see if he could handle the increased level of exercise and if he mentioned the stress symptoms he was experiencing when he met with the doctor. If he says "no" to either or both of these, tell him that you would feel much better if he went ahead and did that. Mention that sometimes precautions pay big dividends, and that you'd really appreciate it if he'd give it some thought.

He keeps putting things off. He could lose everything. What can I do?

Help him see that this is happening. Help him see how it affects other people and how it could eventually damage his career, his marriage, and his friendships. Encourage him to get help finding out what is causing this so he'll have the tools to change it. Point out that if it is something physical, there are treatments. And remind him that the brain is a physical part of the body, too.

She dawdles until it's too late. Everyone's frustrated with her, including herself. What would help?

Tell her you appreciate her frustration. Tell her you share it, not only in terms of what she must be feeling but because you feel it yourself. Let her know you'll do your best to help her get ready, but you don't want to continue to miss things all the time. As hard as it will be to do, leave on time even if she will be left out. In time, this may help her recognize the need to get professional help. And don't feel guilty. As long as you continue to provide love and support—both practical and emotional—you shouldn't consistently give up things that would enrich your personal experience.

He always has excuses. They're not believable anymore. How do I reach him?

Tell him that "excuses" has become his middle name and you'd rather talk about something else. However, reassure him that if there is a way for you to help him avoid the need to make excuses, you'd be happy to talk about that whenever he wants. Let him know that it hurts to watch him have to make excuses all the time and that you know it also hurts him to have to keep making them. If he is seeing a medical professional about it and not getting anywhere, urge him to discuss lack of progress with the person he is seeing, to explore other options, and to consider getting an opinion from someone else.

SHE CAN'T GET ANYTHING DONE. HOW CAN I HELP HER CONCENTRATE?

Anxiety can affect one's ability to focus. It can also consume one's thoughts and take up huge chunks of time. There are a number of things you might suggest. One is keeping a log to help her estimate how much time it actually takes to accomplish something and how much additional time is consumed by anxiety-related thoughts and activities. Then help her plan her time in a way that takes into account both kinds of time. If she is already getting professional help, she should raise the focus issue there. There are approaches professionals can suggest that might help, and if she is on medications they would want to review them. Point out that focus problems are not unusual and that professionals will not be surprised to hear about them. You might also suggest she review her diet and her sleeping patterns. Changes in sleep tend to affect concentration and focus in all of us. The more balanced the diet the better both body and brain can function because they will have the necessary nutrients. This is especially important because anxiety can interfere with sleep and eating habits and she could end up in a vicious cycle where each intensifies the other.

HE WON'T TALK. HOW CAN I GET HIM TO OPEN UP?

You may not be able to. In order for him to feel comfortable enough to open up, he may need to talk to someone who has been where he is and with whom he can feel a different kind of bond. Try to encourage him to find someone he can talk to—family member, friend, professional, a stranger. Depending on whether there is a diagnosis or not, you might want to let him know about support groups or chat groups in which he could participate. Both could be private in nature; the latter could be anonymous as well.

HE KEEPS DOING THE SAME THING OVER AND OVER. I'M WORRIED. AND I JUST DON'T HAVE ANY PATIENCE FOR IT.

This could be a sign of obsessive compulsive disorder. If he is suffering from this form of anxiety, you are probably not the only person who is noticing it, and it is most likely disrupting his life in significant ways. If he has not been evaluated for OCD, it would be a good idea because there are effective treatments.

Though patience is one of the toughest things to sustain when someone you know is suffering from OCD, it may be one of the most important ingredients in your support tool kit. And it's not something you get more of just by wishing for it. Instead of thinking about the patience you need, it may help to think about the repetitive acts in a different way.

Repetition often begins as a form of comfort. We all do this by listening to favorite music over and over or by repeating healing sayings to ourselves. Children will ask for certain books to be read many times over and will go back to toys they've outgrown when they are worried, sad, or sick. Adults will take out memories and revisit them as often as they can when they feel needy. All over the world people turn to prayer and ritual at important times of their lives and at moments of crisis—and they derive comfort from saying words they have said many times before. Prayer is a form of sacred repetition.

For most people, such comfort doesn't become a monster that seizes their minds and goes out of control. It is simply a way to wrap a blanket around themselves when things hurt. But for those susceptible to OCD, what was a source of comfort—and in some ways still is—becomes a force they must submit to.

It's also a need for completion. We go through the motions of an action until it feels complete. For someone with OCD, the switch that gives them that feeling of completion never moves from the open to the closed position. This can be painful, and repetition is a way of trying to force the mechanism to work. This isn't just psychological; it's a physiological response. This search for completion is similar to what happens in music when a phrase seems to end on a seventh chord—that feeling of hanging there, incomplete and unresolved. No one ever leaves it there; the music always comes back to the tonic. A goal of therapy is to establish a shut-off switch.

If you can focus on what the repetition is trying to do, you will find that your stores of patience will multiply.

SHE HAS OCD AND HER LATENESS IS UPSETTING EVERYONE AROUND HER. HOW CAN I HELP HER MAINTAIN HER RELATIONSHIPS?

When people suffer from OCD, all their concentration is on completing their rituals so they can get out the door. Often, it just doesn't occur to them to call to warn people that they will be late. This is something you might be able to help them with because, over time, the people on the receiving end of chronic lateness combined with awkward handling of the situation will get so frustrated they will either explode or bow out. Help the person you care about understand that the people on the receiving end can start to take it personally.

But keep in mind that apologizing after the fact will be much easier for him to incorporate into his ritual than will calling to say that he is going to be late. This is because making a call to say that he is running late is not part of the ritual; in fact, breaking off during a ritual to make such a call can disturb the ritual and force him to start over. Alternatively, adding a "just letting you know my status" call to a ritual—making it a permanent part of the ritual—could make things worse, too. So the possible success of this approach will depend very much on the person, the severity of the OCD, and the type of therapy he is working on with a professional specializing in OCD. That said, don't dismiss it out of hand. Talk it over; try it; suggest that he explore the idea in counseling.

What do I do in the meantime? Ask him if he realizes he's three hours late again!?

If the person you care about is struggling with OCD and his rituals are making him later and later, you may begin to lose patience with him for holding up your plans. He does realize this, and he already feels terrible about it. If you don't know he has OCD, he may not have a way to explain it. If you do know about it, he realizes that you don't grasp the way it takes over, so he still doesn't know what to say. He may try to explain, but he knows whatever he says will sound lame.

What he hears is that you are angry, that you believe he should have developed ways to compensate for the OCD by now, that you think he is unforgivably rude, and that no matter how hard he works to prevent it he is driving you away. This will only encourage him to feel hopeless and to avoid making commitments.

Instead of venting your frustration, try viewing his problem the way you would view an obvious physical disability. If he had a broken leg and it took him much longer to get going and get things done, you'd be able to empathize. You'd recognize that when something isn't working right, other forms of functioning are often affected. You'd understand that healing takes time, treatment and rest, and that some behavioral changes might come with the territory. This is true for OCD, too. OCD is not a choice, it is an illness.

IF AN OLDER PERSON STARTS TO CHECK AND RECHECK THINGS, DOES IT MEAN SHE IS DEVELOPING OCD?

Sometimes, as people grow older, a need to check and recheck things may appear, but it will *not* be a sign of OCD. Instead, it will usually be a sign of some short-term memory loss—not that they have a compulsion to recheck, but that they don't remember if they completed a task. Some of this is quite normal in older people. If this happens a lot, and it is accompanied by other memory issues, there is also the possibility that the person you care about might be in the beginning stages of Alzheimer's disease or be suffering from another form of dementia that can develop as a result of Parkinson's disease, a stroke, or heart surgery.

A need for things to always be in the same place or to be done in the same way can also develop as people grow older. These, too, are ways to compensate for memory shortfalls. By following a pattern, it is more likely that everything that should be done will be done, and that this will happen without having to think about it. By not rearranging cabinets or setting things down in an unaccustomed place, they can rely on long-established memories of where things are. This is not OCD because it is neither a compulsion nor an obsession. It is a preference and a coping strategy that many older people discover for themselves.

SHE BLOWS UP AND OVERREACTS WHEN ONE WOULDN'T EXPECT IT.

This can be an indication of an anxiety disorder, such as a phobia. For example, you might not particularly like spiders or snakes and avoid seeking them out. Yet if for some reason they turn up in your environment, your reaction would be to back away and not touch them. Someone with a phobia, however, may freak in such a way that no one in the room is likely to miss it. If this isn't something you knew about this person, don't try to talk her out of it; just help her get out of the situation as quickly as possible. If you can't move her, get the offending object out of sight, hearing, smell, and conversation. Later, when she has come back to herself, she might be able to talk to you about it.

Blowing up and overreacting could also be a result of posttraumatic stress. If something reminded you of an emotionally difficult time in your past, you might feel annoyed, hurt, even stricken on the inside, but someone suffering from PTSD could start screaming and yelling, could throw something or kick an object across the room. His loss of control might look like a child's tantrum, except that here is an adult in horrible pain who might be reliving a horrible event. He won't be able to tell you what is going on, and he will be so consumed by his own pain and fear that he will not be able to turn it off or even recognize that he is overreacting.

This behavior might also be a panic attack with no specific connection to anything, or it could be OCD and relate to an obsession or compulsion that is being violated by someone else and is so distracting that it is impossible for him to proceed with a conversation or an action or even a thought. In every case, the important thing is to relieve the pressure by removing whatever is causing the outburst or helping the person remove himself from the situation. (See chapter 13 on triggers and flashpoints.)

HE'LL STILL PARTICIPATE IN ANY KIND OF ACTIVITY AROUND THE NEIGHBORHOOD, BUT HE WON'T LEAVE TOWN. SHOULD I BE WORRIED?

If this has been going on for a while, he hasn't been under a crunch at work, and you know he's turning down outings with other people, too, then he might have developed a phobia. It could be a fear of highway driving or bridges. It could be a fear of heights, enclosed spaces, or densely populated areas. Think about where you used to go and see what they have in common. Try suggesting alternatives that wouldn't include, say, elevators or crowds. Offer to be the one who drives and see if that makes a difference. See if he shows some interest or considers them more carefully.

If that doesn't work, ask him what would entice him to leave town. If the answer is nothing, ask if there is anything that has become uncomfortable about going out of town and what you could do to mitigate that. If he entrusts you with what is happening, and it is a phobia, you can help with specific questions, suggestions, and actions:

- "Is there something we can do to make this easier?"
- "If it would help to clutch my arm, the risk of nail marks would be well worth it!"
- "Would it help to take the freight elevator? It's a lot larger."
- "Let's stand near the door so we can be the first ones off."
- "I'd prefer the center lane as we cross the bridge. Let's stay on it all the way."
- "You've borne the brunt of the driving on our trips for years. Why don't I do my share now?"

SHE WON'T GO NEAR THE WATER AT ALL, NOT EVEN TO SUNBATHE. HOW SHOULD I RESPOND?

For some people, a phobia isn't just limited to what *they* can do, it also extends to watching other people. She may be afraid of water—not just going in it or being near it, but of seeing other people wading or swimming or even picnicking near water. Don't force her to go. Don't make her feel ashamed or foolish. Just let her know that if she ever wants to work on this that you'll support her.

WHAT IF I ENCOUNTER SOMETHING THAT LOOKS LIKE ANXIETY, BUT I DON'T KNOW THE PERSON WELL OR THE PERSON IS A STRANGER TO ME?

This can happen in a number of contexts. It could be a situation where someone is panicking and no one is helping. It could be a situation where you are in a position of authority, but you don't know the person's medical history. Maybe you're a tour guide, a police officer, a workshop leader, a referee, or the director of an event. And you see someone freaking out, sweating profusely, talking incoherently, or shaking uncontrollably. It's best not to assume anything. It might be anxiety, and it might not. It could be shock; it could be an insulin reaction; it could be drugs; it could be any number of medical situations. Even if you are a doctor, you might need to conduct an examination and do some tests before reaching a conclusion.

Be conservative in what you do, try to get some information from the person who is exhibiting some symptoms, get some help. And in the meantime, try to take the stress out of the situation by reassuring the person that things are going to be okay and that you'll help. Tell him what you see—shaking, sweating, heavy breathing—and ask what else he is feeling. Ask if this has happened to him before and if he knows what will help. If he can't answer questions, work on calming him first. Work with him on breathing (see chapter 13 on triggers and flashpoints). Ask when he last ate. Ask if he's on any medications. Ask if he's diabetic. Ask if he's missed any medications he should have taken. When in doubt, get him some medical attention to assess the situation.

Part V

*

KIDS AND TEENAGERS

"Time heals what reason cannot."

                     ❧ Seneca

Chapter Seventeen

Tips for Kids

When Someone Close to Them
Suffers from Anxiety

When you live with someone suffering from anxiety, you live with the person *and* with anxiety. This is difficult enough for adults; for kids, it can be frightening as well as confusing.

Some kids are born into a situation in which a parent or sibling is suffering from anxiety. For them, the anxiety is part of the person they know, and the way their household works is the norm. As they grow older and start to spend time at school and in other people's homes, they begin to note distinctions, have questions, and draw conclusions, but they may not know how to respond.

Other kids may instead encounter either an abrupt or gradual change as a family member begins to act differently, unexpectedly, erratically—and then expect different behavior from them, too.

Not surprisingly, kids want to know what is happening, why it is happening, what can be done about it, how long it will take to "fix," whether they had any part in what has happened, how it will affect them in the meantime, what they can do to minimize its effect on their lives, and if there's anything they can do to help.

No matter how old children are, when a member of the family is struggling with anxiety, they suffer, too. The impact on children will depend on the type of anxiety, how severe it is, whether it's a part of their lives every day or only becomes obvious once in a while. It will depend on a child's personality and temperament, how the anxiety is explained, the kinds of support surrounding the child. If the person with anxiety and the child have a close relationship, it will also depend on their maintaining that closeness.

This chapter focuses on how to talk to kids about someone close to them who is suffering from anxiety. It suggests some ways to initiate the discussion, answers some common questions children often have about anxiety, and offers some strategies they could use to cope.

BRINGING UP THE TOPIC

If the change is abrupt, someone should take the children aside and explain what is happening and what it means to them. The first step is to acknowledge that something is happening.

- "I know you noticed some changes, and I thought you might want to know what's going on. Let's sit down and I'll try to explain things."
- "Things have been a little weird lately, and you must have a lot of questions. I'd like to try to answer them."
- "It's been a little rough the last few days, hasn't it? And you've been a real trooper. Let's talk about it, okay?"

If the change is gradual, or the behavior has always been there, it's sometimes best to wait for an opening that a child provides and ease into the subject that way.

- "This is something that bothers you, isn't it?"
- "I get the feeling you've wondered about that. Fire away."
- "It's okay to be upset, you know."
- "It can get to me, too. It's just hard."

WHAT IS IT? WHY IS IT HAPPENING?

When children ask this question, remind them that there are all kinds of ways to get sick: colds, sore throats, laryngitis, headaches, stomachaches. Maybe they've had poison ivy or strep throat or ear infections and needed medicine to get better. Someone they know might have had a broken arm or leg and been in a cast for a long time. Tell them that this is similar and that in this case, too, it might take a long time for the person to get better.

This might be enough for a very young child. An older child might want some more information, such as what this is called (anxiety) and how it works. You might want to talk about the form it takes even if children don't ask for a specific name. If it's generalized anxiety disorder, you could talk about a general feeling of unease that is more than just nervousness and, though it's not clear where it comes from, there are ways to make it better. If it's phobia with a precipitating cause, you could mention it, but add that actually there doesn't have to be anything that happened for someone to develop the phobia. If it's a phobia that would only show itself occasionally, you can provide reassurance that it won't be a big part of family life. If it's a phobia that will affect everyday life, talk about the treatment that is available and how you will all manage in the meantime.

Give them a chance to ask questions, and answer those they raise, but don't give them more information than they want. When they are ready for more information, or need it, they will come to you for it, particularly if you tell them to let you know if there is anything else they think of to ask later.

The questions of why this is happening and where it comes from are among those questions to answer once they ask them. Older children will want more complete answers. This is because they may be afraid that you, too, could develop anxiety, and because they may wonder about getting it themselves. Assure them that anxiety is not contagious like a cold, so it is not something they can "catch." And tell them that its causes are not clear. Sometimes it might start because of something that has happened that was frightening or traumatic. Yet, for many people, those feelings would not develop into anxiety.

Discuss with them the theory that some people might be more likely to develop anxiety than others, and that it might be a vulnerability or sensitivity they are born with. However, assure them that just because they are born with it doesn't mean it will ever happen to them. Make sure they know that there are a number of diseases that people can be genetically vulnerable to, yet many people never develop those diseases during their lifetimes.

WILL SHE GET BETTER?

When kids ask this question, tell them "Yes." Because anxiety disorders are highly treatable, if a person seeks out professional help and follows through on it, the chances are very good that her life can come back to normal or close to it. This could take a number of months to happen, there might still be some things she might need to accommodate for, and sometimes the anxiety could recur, but it's fair to paint a positive picture.

What's important is letting kids know that it's very possible to get better, that you and the person suffering from it are both working hard at it, that you have a doctor's help, and that all of you—adults and kids—are going to get through this as you have other things in your lives. Recovering isn't something that happens very fast or right away, and it could take a while to begin to see a difference. So it is very worthwhile for everyone to just hang in there.

WHAT CAN I DO?

When kids want to help, there are a number of things you can suggest. You might say:

- "The best thing you can do is keep on loving him no matter what."
- "If she wants company, try to spend some time with her when you can. If she wants to be alone, give her some space. If you're not sure what she would prefer, ask. Just as you don't feel the same about what you want all the time, neither will she."
- "Maybe you could distract him in some way. Offer to play a game, or tell him about your day. See if he'd like to watch a movie with you."
- "Be patient."
- "Show him respect."
- "Ask her advice on something."
- "Admit you get scared sometimes."
- "He may want to talk to you about how he is feeling, about what is happening. It may be hard for you to listen to this, but think about how much he must love and respect you to trust you with this and want to explain it to you. You don't have to say much to him in response. Just tell him how hard it sounds or how much you love him or what a great father you think he is. Maybe hold his hand or hug him and smile at him. It's okay to cry and say you hurt for him and wish for him to get better soon. Whatever feels right at the time."
- "A great thing to do—but only if you are comfortable with it—is to introduce a friend to him and tell both of them how much you wanted them to meet each other. This is showing him how much you love and respect him and that you are not ashamed or embarrassed about his illness."

IS IT MY FAULT?

Make it very clear that it is absolutely not the child's fault. Even if the person she cares about has post-traumatic stress and the child was part of the situation that contributed to it, the disorder is still not in any way the child's fault. Compare it to other situations in life. For example, what if she'd carried home from school a germ for flu and someone in her family caught it? Would that be her fault? Of course not. She couldn't control being exposed to the germ, or control having it on her, or control whether her father caught it or not, or control whether he could beat it easily or not. And it wouldn't be her father's fault either. It's no one's fault; it just is.

You might also explain that the same thing is true for the anxiety disorder. The person who has it didn't cause it, is not at fault for getting it, and is not at fault for having a hard time overcoming it. Some things are much tougher than others to deal with.

WHAT SHOULD I SAY?

Older kids may avoid the person with anxiety, particularly if it is an adult. They may admit that they just don't know what to say, or that they've gotten irritable themselves and snapped at the person who is struggling. If they give you the opening, you can talk to them about things they could say. Once they try a few suggestions, they will be more comfortable about generating their own conversation. Here are some things they could try:

- "Hey, I love you anyway."
- "Sometimes I just don't know what to say."
- "I'm sorry I lost it. This is just so hard sometimes."
- "I guess it's hard for you, too, isn't it?"

- "I know you are working very hard at not being afraid. Well, I'm working hard on that myself. Know what I mean?"
- "I remember how things were. I want them to be like that again. I'm glad you are getting help with this."
- "I'm glad you're my Dad, though sometimes I just get so mad!"
- "I know he's my little brother, but sometimes this doesn't seem real."
- "You're my Mom, no matter what."
- "I'm really trying, but I've still got to be me."

DEALING WITH IT

Kids' concerns tend to fall into two categories: How can their lives go on in as normal a fashion as possible, and how should they react to things the person with anxiety says, does, or expects when it's not what they are used to, or it doesn't make sense, or it makes them very uncomfortable. There are a number of things you can do to help kids cope with these.

Maintain routine as much as possible

Not only parents and family members, but teachers, guidance counselors, coaches, principals, and neighbors can help to preserve the day-to-day routine. They can do this by going on with regular activities, treating the child in the same way, being matter-of-fact about things that come up—not making a big deal of them, yet being empathetic and in a problem-solving mode. Being aware of this stress in the child's life doesn't mean adults have to dwell on it; it does mean they can quietly make accommodations, be flexible, and say something supportive as appropriate. Most of the time, they can best support the child by helping things go on as usual. This gives kids a sense of stability and security; it makes them feel safe.

Prepare kids for changes

If there are two adults in the household and one of them is suffering from anxiety, the adult who doesn't have anxiety can promise to keep a child's life on as even a keel as possible: school, bedtimes, meals, activities, time with friends will stay pretty much as usual. That adult should explain, though, that all those things might not happen in exactly the same way. For example, there might be more car pools, time with friends might have to happen at the friend's house more often than at home, and getting to show up at every game or performance to cheer and clap might not always be possible.

The fact is that the person who is ill might need more help and attention than usual, might need help keeping appointments with doctors or therapists. Also, if the person who is ill can't work as many hours, there might be less money for a while. This could mean cutting back on some things, or it could mean that the other adult must start working or might work longer hours. Kids will appreciate being told all this—not only for the reassurance that they need, but because telling them what might happen and why is a mark of respect.

Explain these things in general terms and promise to keep them posted. Not being left in the dark will make them feel a part of the solution, and this will help them to be accommodating and flexible as things change around them.

Explain your own grumpiness

Also, you need to let them know that, even though you are not the person suffering from anxiety, you may feel overwhelmed, worried, and extra tired at times, and that this could make you get grumpy, irritable, and impatient. Make sure they understand that if you act like that with them, it might not have anything to do with anything they are doing. It could just have to do with the way you feel. Tell them you are apologizing ahead of time for when that happens, and ask them to please forgive you ahead of time, too. And tell them you'll try to warn them if you realize that you're in a particularly grumpy mood so that they'll be prepared.

Talk about ways to interact

The second part of their concern is more difficult to address because in a way it's what this whole book addresses. It's only fair to agree that one doesn't always know what to say or do in response to anxiety. Tell her to do the best she can. Tell her that, although this is hard to understand, someone struggling with anxiety can get stuck in what he is thinking and just can't help it. That he would rather be as he was before, that he watches himself doing it and feels terrible about it, and that he also feels terrible about how his friends and family feel about it, too.

Suggest that she try to ignore what can be ignored, that she treat him with as much respect as she can, find patience wherever she can find it, and let him know how much she loves him anyway—even if he is confusing her and frustrating her sometimes.

Give them some perspective

Remind kids that when they are sick, they tend to be grumpy, irritable, impatient, demanding, unreasonable, too. And that, unfortunately, feeling sick doesn't get any easier just because one is an adult.

Help them remember what it is like to have strong feelings that hurt or make them angry or afraid and how good it is to have ways they've learned to calm themselves down: maybe by cuddling a stuffed animal, or crying, taking a walk, picking up a book, tackling some chores, working on a hobby, listening to music. Explain that sometimes people can lose the ability to calm themselves and need help to learn new ways or relearn old ones, especially when the feelings are stronger than ever. For younger children, you might say something along these lines:

- "Your mommy is having a hard time with her feelings."
- "When your brother gets scared he gets angry, and that doesn't really help him make the scared feeling go away."
- "You do a good job of rocking your bear when you feel scared and that helps you calm down. Your sister can't do that right now, but she'll feel better when she learns how. That might take a while and we are going to help her."
- "Sometimes you withdraw and hide out in your room, or just don't want to talk to anyone or do anything. Sometimes that helps you regroup; sometimes you need help to get back out there. The same could be true for your dad, but it could be a much more intense feeling, and it might take a while for him to get there even with help."

You might also remind them that their lives are still centered around school, activities, homework, chores, other commitments, and sleep. Sometimes it can help give them perspective when they realize that they only interact with the person suffering from anxiety one or two hours out of twenty-four.

Ask how you can help

With school-age kids, you can ask what bothers them the most and what would help them the most. Tell them you'll do your best to help them work out the first and provide the second. The more specific they are, the better you'll be able to help, but keep in mind that it may be hard for them to be specific. If that's the case, help them out. Ask them if there are particular things they want to be able to do or places they want to go. Ask them if it would help to have some special time with you every day, even if it's only for a few minutes. Ask them if combining that time with driving somewhere together or with a bedtime ritual would be okay. Ask if it's their interactions with the person suffering from anxiety that's most difficult and whether it's easier for them to do that one-on-one or with someone else as part of the conversation.

It won't be the same for everyone. Find out if there are specific types of situations that are more difficult and why: Is it because they don't know what to say, or don't want to feel as if they are staring, or don't know how to act as if everything's the same, or something else. Then try to talk out the details and come up with a plan that might work. Consider acting it out with them to see how it feels. Tell them to let you know how it worked out in "real life" so that you can work together to fine-tune it. All this lets them know that you are there for them, that you are confident you'll all get through this, and that life can still be good in the meantime.

With preschoolers, let them take the lead. Just be sure to give them more hugs, tell them how much you love them, let them know what a great job they are doing with something they've tackled. Give them a chance to bring up their concerns. If it's their father who suffers from anxiety, you can open the door by mentioning how much Dad loves them. If it's a sibling who has anxiety, you can open the door by telling them how good a friend they are to their brother or sister. Don't go on to something else right away. Let there be a natural pause in the conversation for a while. If they bring up a concern, be prepared to answer it tenderly but matter-of-factly. Invite them to say more—either then or later—by saying you're glad they brought it up.

Because you will be busier and more preoccupied yourself, you might consider enlisting other kinds of support. Perhaps a grown sibling, an uncle or aunt, a godparent, or the parent of a close friend could spend extra time or start calling on a regular basis. Perhaps there is a support group for children who are dealing with anxiety in the family. Kids will welcome the extra positive attention, the time to talk about what's bothering them, and especially a safe time and place to vent when everything gets to be too much for them.

It's also a good idea to talk to them about venting. They need to know that there's nothing wrong with getting angry, sad, frustrated, or scared, and that it's good to have a way to deal with those emotions.

SEE THE SITUATION FROM A CHILD'S POINT OF VIEW

It's important to remember that a parent's anxiety could prevent a child from having a full life. The other parent and other adults in the child's life can work to make sure that the parent struggling with anxiety doesn't end up crippling his child with his own fears. Let kids learn to swim and enjoy summer activities with their friends. Let them go mountain climbing. They can learn precautions, but they shouldn't have unwarranted restrictions, or be taught to be anxious or afraid. If this happens, they will resent the restrictions and suffer unnecessary fears.

It's also helpful to be aware of kids' potential embarrassment about their parents. As kids move into their teen years, they tend to be embarrassed about their parents anyway. But when a parent is suffering from anxiety, their embarrassment may be quite different. It is your stance, your composure, your continued respect for the person with anxiety, and your matter-of-fact inclusion of that person in all sorts of activities with friends and strangers that will help kids be able to reach the same place in their minds with regard to their friends. For some kids, this will be very hard, especially if the symptoms of anxiety are obvious and the atmosphere at home is tense and gloomy. This, too, is something you can talk to them about, but mostly, be patient. Overcoming embarrassment could take them a while, and if you remember what being a kid was like—and how nerve-racking it was even to bring home a date without something like anxiety in the picture—you should be able to understand.

"My knowledge is pessimistic, but my willing and hoping are optimistic."

❧ ALBERT SCHWEITZER

Chapter Eighteen

What About Kids

કુ

WHEN THEY SUFFER FROM ANXIETY THEMSELVES

Kids, too, can suffer from anxiety. It is estimated that 13 percent of children aged nine to seventeen suffer from an anxiety disorder. When children under the age of nine are included in the estimation, it is possible that 10 percent of all children could be suffering from anxiety.

Deciding whom to include in the studies that generate these kinds of statistics is a little more difficult when studying children than when studying adults. One reason is that children don't always make good reporters when asked questions, and their parents aren't always good observers. This is not surprising, because it can be hard to be objective and have perspective about one's children. Another reason is that anxiety-like issues can be normal in certain situations for young children, and they can outgrow them. This makes it difficult to know whether to include them in studies and statistics about anxiety.

But it is important to keep in mind that anxiety can affect kids as easily as it can adults. Too often, anxiety disorders appear in childhood but are not recognized until kids grow up. Specific phobias, for example, can start at any time and can occur because of something that has actually happened, or be influenced by a movie or someone else's fear. OCD often starts in childhood or adolescence, but a diagnosis can take eight to twelve years on average. This gives the illness and the strategies one uses to hide it a long time to become embedded.

The focus of this chapter is to help you understand when a child might be suffering from anxiety, to help you talk to him about it, and to offer suggestions on how to provide the support he will need. This chapter is important because, though symptoms can overlap, childhood anxiety doesn't always look like the anxiety adults are struggling with. And because, if an adult in the family is suffering from a form of anxiety, a child in the family might be vulnerable, too.

SOME SYMPTOMS OF CHILDHOOD ANXIETY

Generally, when a child is suffering from a form of anxiety—for example, generalized anxiety disorder or social anxiety disorder—you will likely see additional symptoms such as nightmares or vomiting the night before a stressful event. You won't necessarily see fear or worry, though you might still see these or other things you associate with anxiety. This is because, with children, what you are most likely to see are changes in behavior. When these changes are persistent, not just a one-time thing, it's worth taking a second look.

Kids are always changing—that's part of growing up and developing. The changes to be concerned about are those that take away from the quality of their lives or even affect their ability to function. Sometimes these changes are their way of dealing with anxiety, but just as with adults, some of their ways of coping could actually be making their lives more difficult rather than less so. Here are some things to look for when you consider a change in behavior and wonder whether you need to be worried about it. If your child is a teen, some items on the list may sound like things teens do anyway. But if these behaviors are persistent, more extreme than usual, or they are exhibiting several of them, then anxiety may have entered the picture. In any case, don't jump to conclusions. It might be anxiety and it might not. It's not your job to diagnose what is wrong, only to realize that something might need to be checked out and to help find someone qualified to do that.

Signs to look for when you suspect childhood anxiety

- Have they stopped getting together with friends?
- Have they stopped engaging in normal social activities with other kids?
- Is something getting in the way of going to school, doing homework, completing projects, participating in class, academic performance in general, grades in particular, etc.?
- Do they avoid activities they used to engage in, hobbies or sports or other extracurricular activities they were involved in?
- Have their everyday routines changed drastically?
- Are they afraid to be away from home?
- Are they getting a lot of headaches, stomachaches, or other aches and pains?
- Do they seem much more clingy, needy, restless, tense, or uneasy?
- Do they worry all the time, seem fearful, feel dread, sweat a lot, seem hyperreactive, or sensitive?
- Are there other areas in which they used to function well but no longer do?
- Have they changed the way they interact with people?
- Do they have trouble concentrating or following directions, or do they seem to get distracted easily?
- Do they avoid people, events, places, or topics of conversation?

- Do they seem to shut down?
- Do they appear to be hiding things and denying that anything is wrong? (This could also be a sign of substance abuse, or a sign that this is how they are trying to cope.)
- Do they get angry and stay angry most of the time? Are they constantly irritable, or do they throw tantrums? (For teens, that could be a sign of substance abuse, the use of street drugs, etc. Again, it could be how they are trying to cope.)

It may not be the parent who sees these things. If teachers complain that he won't pay attention, can't concentrate, gets easily frustrated or teary, and doesn't bounce back, or a coach comes down on her because she is easily distracted, unwilling to try new drills, unable to follow directions, unable to proceed (frozen/paralyzed), or uncaring (because she stopped showing up), don't immediately jump on your kids. It may be that those are symptoms of anxiety, or something else, such as depression. And it's also important to realize that they could be hurting and confused and even embarrassed because they don't know where their behaviors are coming from. Some of the things kids do to cope with their anxiety are deliberate and conscious (refusing to go to school), some of them are unconscious (getting stomachaches), and with some they don't even see the connection (drinking or drugs).

WHAT ELSE COULD IT BE?

Many kids will go through anxious times when dealing with new social situations or separation from their parents—this is a normal part of growing up. In this case, the anxiousness they feel does not rise to the level of a clinical disorder and, even when they show symptoms sufficient to meet diagnostic criteria, they will work through it. For most kids, feeling anxious is a natural part of development that occurs at points of change in their lives—when they need to deal with something new and different—and they will transition through it.

For young children it could be the first day of school, entering kindergarten, swimming class, or going away to camp. What they need most are parents who will support them through the process and encourage them.

For older children it could be the switch to middle school or high school. There's a lot of stress involved when adjusting to a new situation, being at the bottom of a pecking order, and being in an environment with many more kids. Many kids have a tough time at first and may react severely for several weeks. But in both cases, once children have learned new social skills, made friends, become comfortable in the situation, the anxiety goes away. These situations are part of finding one's place in the world and may cause some kids more stress than others. This happens because they don't have enough reservoirs of experience in terms of what they have observed, experienced, understood, or mastered, and because they are still developing coping skills for situations like this.

Also, sudden changes and eccentricities don't necessarily mean adolescents and teens have developed an anxiety disorder. Remember that this is a time of experimentation and peer pressure—needing to fit in as well as needing to try out different identities.

Maybe he suddenly refuses to wear anything but black pants, and it goes on for months. This doesn't mean he has developed OCD. It could just be "being a kid." Maybe it's an unconscious way to control something in his life when he is just beginning to realize how much is uncontrollable, even for adults. Maybe it's a comfort not to have to choose what pants to wear every day, or he knows everything goes with black, so this simplifies his life. He could be trying to assert his individuality or it could be that he just likes black and wants to go with it for now.

Most of the time, if he wants to wear black pants every day, as long as the other areas of his life appear okay, it'll probably pass and you can leave it alone. In the same way, if she wants to eat the same lunch every day, ignore it. Don't make an issue of it.

But if something they are doing (or refusing to do) interferes with or stops them from participating in activities, or if it starts to build up into a multileveled ritual that takes a lot of time, or if challenges to that ritual or routine lead to repeated meltdowns, then it's worthwhile to take some steps to address it.

STEPS TO TAKE

If you are concerned that a child might be suffering from anxiety, first try to sit down and talk to him or her about it. See if something else could be going on. Maybe there's a bully at school; perhaps his clothes are a passport to inclusion with other kids, a sort of uniform; maybe there is some idiosyncratic reason similar to why someone would play a certain song over and over without getting tired of it.

However, if a child confides that she doesn't know why she is doing what she's doing, or he says he wishes he could change his behavior, or she says these changes are making her sad, uneasy, or stressed out, then you can say you're going to think about how to help. At the same time, ask "How can I help right now?" Whether he acknowledges that something is wrong, denies there is a problem, or insists nothing has changed, you need to listen to your gut. If you think something isn't right, check it out.

The second step is to confer with the pediatrician and set up an appointment. Tell her what you are seeing. Tell her what he is saying. Say you're concerned and would appreciate an evaluation.

Then have a conversation with your child about the appointment you've made. Explain that the doctor can give a physical the way she usually does and, depending on what she sees and on what he tells her, she'll be able to make some suggestions. That she has experience with a lot of kids and that he'll be able to benefit from that.

The conversation might be a little different with a five-year-old than with a twelve-year-old, but the principle is the same. You may not need to say anything more before setting up the appointment. Just as in other situations, you can be guided in what you say by what your child actually asks. If your child seems to need more reassurance, some things you could say might be:

- "When we're not sure what to do, we consult someone who does. It could be a teacher or a coach, a librarian or financial advisor, an electrician or an architect, a fashion designer or a hairdresser. In this case it's a doctor. Someone with experience and training who might be able to give us advice and help."
- "We'll do this together."
- "You shouldn't have to feel this way all the time, and we're going to find out how to change that."
- "If you couldn't see the blackboard very well or started getting a lot of headaches, one of the things the doctor would check would be your eyes. If you didn't have twenty-twenty vision, he'd write you a prescription for glasses, and those symptoms would go away. Sometimes there are simple solutions that can make life so much better. Let's give the doctor a chance to do something like that."

You want to come to them with great confidence and let them hear in your voice that you are not frightened by this.

If you are a family friend, you will not be able to insist he see his doctor. If you are his parent or guardian, even if he resists going, it's still your obligation and responsibility to get him the best help you can, and to start by uncovering what is going on. You can explain that to him, too.

Third, if the pediatrician suspects that he is suffering from depression or anxiety, then it's a good idea to be referred to a mental health professional who can make a more precise diagnosis. Because children are not miniature adults, pediatricians will often refer to someone who specializes in child and/or adolescent mental health and who is trained in how the symptoms present and in how kids will compensate. That person can get a family history, get to know the parents, determine if there is anything that runs in the family that might give a hint to what is going on, ask if they've seen these kinds of behaviors before, and find out if the child has been in any ongoing stressful situations at school, at home, or in one of his activities. All of these help in making a diagnosis.

MAJOR CONCERNS KIDS HAVE

Sometimes it is the school that observes something and calls. Kids often feel they must have done something wrong, or they may feel very exposed, embarrassed, humiliated, ashamed. It's important to reassure them that they haven't done anything wrong, that teachers are trained to look out for things like this, and that you'll help them take care of this so school will get better. Especially important is reassuring them about other kids noticing if they bring it up. Tell them that most kids are much too busy with their own stuff to pay attention to anyone else.

Don't forget that kids want to be like everyone else. They don't want to be weird or different, or to look as if they are weird or different, and will do anything to hide anything about themselves that they think would fall into these categories.

Because they don't want to be labeled, they probably won't want to go for any kind of mental health treatment or special ed. They fear that other kids will reject them, ridicule them, harass them, and lump them into a catch-all category as "crazy."

All of this will make it very hard for you to get them to accept treatment.

WHAT MAKES IT HARDER?

Even if you can persuade them to see a doctor or to get counseling, sometimes kids will resist taking medications. They may refuse to take them and tell you so or, to simplify their lives and avoid being nagged, might just pretend to take them. It could be that they don't like the side effects. It's important for them to know that medications can be adjusted or changed and that it can sometimes take a while to find what works best. Encourage them to be partners in the process.

Some kids will resist taking medications altogether. To them, the need to take medications implies that something is very wrong. And actually taking the medications would mean they are accepting that something is wrong with them. It's not a matter of not liking meds or not believing they will work. It's a form of denial, and it is very powerful. Even though on one level they understand that not taking the meds could lead to their anxiety getting worse, they would rather get worse than accept that something is wrong.

In their logic, if they can continue to handle the problem themselves, then it can't be so bad. If, however, they take the medicine and it "fixes" the problem, this will prove that there was something to fix—that something is very wrong with them. They'd rather not deal with that because it will change how they think about themselves.

This kind of thinking doesn't just happen with anxiety. Kids often react this way to other ailments, too. They resist taking insulin, or medicine for seizure disorders such as epilepsy, even though they could end up in the hospital or have a seizure in front of their friends.

Adults can be leery of a diagnosis of anxiety, too. With adults, however, it often helps for them to understand that anxiety is a physical disorder, that it just happens to be of the brain and not of the pancreas or heart or leg. For kids, this is often neither an effective argument nor a relief. Kids tend to feel that nothing really bad can happen to them. And no matter what, they don't want to lose this feeling or risk having it threatened.

The more severe the symptoms, the easier it is to get someone to accept treatment. They clearly see the benefits when they realize they don't have a life anymore, or if they do end up in the hospital and have a close call. Sometimes that's what ends up turning things around. Whereas, when it's moderate, when they think they can manage, or that it will go away, or that other people won't realize what's happening, they will resist doing anything that could help them. Counseling can help them see the benefits of taking necessary medications and help them work through their feelings.

HOW KIDS COMPENSATE

Ironically, though they don't want to take medications prescribed by a doctor, they may decide to self-medicate through street drugs or alcohol. They don't see the irony of this; they see this as taking charge and as proof that there really isn't anything wrong. And if it seems to work, they see that as evidence that they can take care of themselves.

Thus, they can get drawn into substance abuse as a form of coping. They don't realize how hard it will be to stop drinking or taking drugs, that the anxiety will make it harder for them than it would be for someone else, and that they could end up with two problems instead of one. And they don't realize something else: that instead of making them feel better, drugs and alcohol could actually intensify the very symptoms they are trying to push away.

This will be difficult for the adults in their lives because kids will resist listening to this information. It will also be difficult because the adults in their lives may not understand what they are dealing with. Are the kids they care about using drugs as a matter of experimentation or rebellion, or are they taking them in an effort to control their anxiety? How can an adult tell if someone is suffering from anxiety or is simply high? Or does it just look like they are suffering from anxiety because they are cutting back their use of drugs and are going through withdrawal?

For parents, friends, teachers, coaches, school counselors, and administrators, this can be difficult to interpret. Providing information in a neutral way, sitting down to talk about the possibilities, and bringing someone else into the process are all ways to begin to address what is going on. (For more on substance abuse, see the end of chapter 1.)

How adults can help

The important thing is for parents not to appear frightened. That they be matter-of-fact, empathetic, and make practical suggestions. If it is a kind of transitional social anxiety, be reassuring. Tell them that this is natural and normal and part of growing up and learning how to anticipate and handle new situations.

- "I know it's frightening, but it won't stay that way."
- "It's new now. But it won't always be new."
- "You'll figure things out, and a lot of the other kids are going to be doing the same thing."

Give them anecdotes about *your* childhood. Tell them most people go through this in one way or another. That grown-ups can have this recur when they start a new job or move into a new town. That as they grow up, they'll find it will help to know they've gotten through this before, and they will have learned things to do and say—even things to say to themselves.

On the other hand, if you've gone through the steps and have been referred to a therapist who diagnoses an anxiety disorder, let that person guide you in how best to support your child. Continue to show your child how much you love him, how much you admire her, how you respect the things he does, how you see a whole person. And be careful about some of the words you use when you offer support.

Words to watch out for
- Stay away from the word "fix" because it implies there is something wrong.
- Stay away from the word "blame" because it suggests kids are responsible for what is happening.
- Stay away from the word "fault" because you want to stress that this is something one treats, and is no more your child's fault than catching a cold.
- Don't say, "This is your responsibility"—even if you mean to say you need to work on this together. They'll hear those words, internalize them, and shut down.

Words to keep
- "We'll work on this together."
- "We'll get the help we need and learn what to do."
- "As your mom, I'll do everything I can do to help you, because I know this is scary."

- "As your dad, I'm going to be there all the way, because I know this is unnerving."
- "The more you can tell us about what is happening, when it happens, and other stuff that is happening at the same time, the more effectively we can help."
- "Help us understand how it feels so we can be there for you."
- Reinforce the bond you have by using the word "we."

WHAT HAPPENS AS THEY GROW UP

Some children will outgrow anxiety as they develop confidence in their ability to manage new situations and as they build up successes. Others can learn to manage their anxiety—to use positive and constructive coping strategies, to pay attention to what is happening inside them so they can address what is happening right away. Maybe they'll use medication, cognitive or behavioral therapy, maintenance therapy, relaxation therapies, or something else, or a combination of approaches. What is important is that they know what's available to them and have the confidence to seek them out if they need them.

As teens leave home for work, for college, to marry, and begin to live independently from their families, they should be encouraged to continue to manage their anxiety. Remind them that if they keep on with the techniques they have learned, their lives will be rich. Tell them they shouldn't be shy about seeking help as soon as they feel that something is slipping, because it is always easier to make adjustments sooner rather than later, and that the adjustments are more likely to be minor if they stop the slide at the top of the hill. Reassure them that you will always be available to provide support when they need it, or to help them regain perspective, and that you want them to feel comfortable about asking. They need to know that they can have good lives.

AN IMPORTANT NOTE

Even with all this information, even with a lot of training, child-hood anxiety can be difficult to recognize. As we discussed earlier, part of this is because some of it is the type of situational anxiety that kids outgrow as they gain experience and social skills, and part of it is because at certain stages—such as adolescence—they are dealing with a lot of things at once that can create understand-able levels of stress. But there are other reasons why childhood anxiety often goes unrecognized. Part of it is because children are changeable, and they don't always show the same symptoms in the same way. And part of it is they do their best not to let you see any-thing that they themselves suspect is wrong. And there is a fifth reason. What can make it particularly hard to recognize is that anxiety will often look like depression in kids.

It's important for a professional to tease out that a child is ac-tually suffering from anxiety so that appropriate therapy and treatment can be provided. Otherwise, treatment won't be effec-tive. So if your gut tells you something is wrong, even if your mind can't pin down what makes you feel that way, make sure you go through the steps and consult someone who can help you assess the situation.

Part VI

❧

Taking Care of Yourself

"Little things are often filled with great beauty."

⇛ RALPH WALDO EMERSON

Chapter Nineteen

Living with Stress

༄

Keeping Yourself Whole

*T*his section is about you. Not your role. Not the boundaries you need to establish. Not what you can do for the person you care about. It's about what you can do for yourself.

You need to do the same things for yourself that you are doing for others. Replenish yourself. Find positive ways to view the world. Affirm positive things about yourself. Create oases of calm and peace in your day.

You should do this for yourself no matter what, but when you've taken on the role of helping someone who is suffering, it is even more important. There are always aspects of life that take our energy as well as aspects of life that give us energy. Caring for someone who is suffering can do both because there are always rewards, even if at first it is only the process that is rewarding rather than the results. But the day-to-day reality is an enormous draw on emotional energy, and you will feel that draw as physical exhaustion as well as emotional exhaustion. This is because the suffering alone will hurt you and deplete your energy even if you don't actually take on much of a supportive role. And your desire to see improvement that can't come right away, your feeling of inadequacy when you're not sure what to do, and your concerns about fulfilling your other responsibilities at the same time all continue to take energy.

So you need to put that energy back and make that an ongoing process. You need to find perspective so that things can be relaxed and flowing instead of always a matter of urgency and tension.

MAKE A LIST

We all have experienced times when we've felt incredible bursts of energy, a luscious feeling of relaxation, or an amazing sense of calm and peace. Ask yourself when these have happened. Were you in a particular place? With particular people? Was it after an activity? Did these times have anything in common?

Make separate lists for each of these. For some people, each list will have a distinct set of characteristics. For others, there will be a lot of overlap.

RE-CREATE THE CIRCUMSTANCES

Once you know when in your life you've felt most calm, most at peace, most in wonder, and with the greatest reserves of energy, then you should be able to generate these feelings again. All you have to do is re-create the circumstances. You don't have to set up elaborate get-togethers, go on fancy trips, or wait for a vacation. You don't need to set aside huge amounts of time—which means you'll never do it anyway. Focus on the simple things that made these feelings happen. It's unlikely that huge amounts of money, time, or planning were the key elements.

PENCIL IN THE TIME

What is key is that you allow time for yourself. Time to do nothing. Time to do something else. Time just to enjoy, relax, daydream, sleep. Time to be with someone who nurtures *you*. You not only need this time, you deserve it. And when you restore yourself, you are better able to create positive feelings for someone else.

Make sure these moments of replenishment happen in your

life. Plan for them. Give yourself ten minutes each day, a two-hour chunk weekly, and if possible, an entire day once a month or a weekend once a quarter to do that. You make appointments for other things; treat this the same way. Put those two-hour chunks and days and weekends on your calendar. Make the ten-minute oasis a part of your daily routine. Where's it going to come from? Maybe one phone call will be shorter; maybe you'll cook something less complicated; maybe you'll get up ten minutes earlier each day; maybe you'll do a less important chore three days a week instead of seven; maybe you'll find that ten minutes at work. Ten minutes can be found, even if you lock yourself in the bathroom to get it. And you might even institute a new family tradition in which everyone deliberately takes ten minutes to themselves to recharge—no interruptions allowed.

Ten minutes sound short, but they can accomplish a lot. Think of it as six hundred seconds and it will feel like the gift it is. A gift to yourself.

SOME WAYS TO RELAX AND RECHARGE

The best things to do are the ones that work for you, but here are a few examples that work for others to give you a head start. Set a timer for the amount of time you can take, but take off your watch so you can't watch the seconds tick by. Think of the time as timeless.

- Linger over a cup of coffee.
- Luxuriate in a bath.
- Settle in a rocking chair.
- Relax, eyes closed, with cucumber slices, a wet compress, or a lavender sachet on your eyelids.
- Put something beautiful in view—flowers, a sunset, a painting, rich fabric.
- Sit outside and inhale the air.

- Bask in sunshine.
- Visualize a rainbow, fireworks display, or a special moment, and reexperience all the details through memory.
- Stretch your legs and take a walk.
- Do some yoga.
- Exercise vigorously.
- Take a catnap.
- Soothe yourself with soup.
- Read a favorite passage.
- Envelop yourself with music.
- Surround yourself with an aroma you love. It could be perfume, something special baking in the oven, a candle, cinnamon simmering on the stove.
- Give yourself a treat.
- Make a small change you've always wanted to make.
- Reach out for a hug.
- Play a quick game with someone you love (cards, a board game, an electronic game, shooting hoops, hopscotch, etc.).
- Learn meditation or another relaxation technique.
- Hold hands with someone you love.
- Cuddle.
- Rub your neck and shoulders; massage your hands and calves.
- Lie down and imagine receiving a back rub.
- Soak your feet.
- Take a walk and smile at those you see; feel the warmth of the smiles you receive in return.

The list is endless.

INVESTING SECONDS

Penciling these things in is an extension of something you already do—making appointments, setting up meetings, planning a schedule, consulting your calendar. This makes it relatively easy to incorporate these blocks of time into your way of life.

What is more difficult is changing your behavior on an ongoing basis, from minute to minute, throughout the day. If you can learn to respond to stress as it starts to build, you will be able to take control of it right away and build a habit of resilience. Awareness, perspective, and learning to act right away are the three elements that will help you do this.

Awareness is when you become attuned to your blood racing, stomach tightening, neck or jaw tensing, eyes feeling pressure, breathing growing shallower, voice pitch becoming slightly higher, speech rate getting faster, skin crawling, or that you are not quite listening to what someone is saying to you.

Perspective is when you can ask yourself if the way you use the next twenty seconds will matter when you look back at your day this evening, a month from now, a year from now.

Acting right away to head off stress requires just twenty-second increments of your time. Take twenty seconds for some deep breaths, twenty seconds to close your eyes, or twenty seconds to chuckle at something and make a mental note to share the chuckle with someone else.

Just twenty seconds—count them as you do it—and you will gain minutes and hours of peace, productivity, and prolonged good health. If you pause to do this thirty times during the course of a day, it will only "cost" you a total of ten minutes, but the rewards will be immeasurable. You will multiply your energy.

After you've counted out the twenty seconds a number of times, you will have a memory for how long twenty seconds lasts, and won't have to count them anymore. Then they will have even more impact.

Reassuring yourself

Your energy may not be the only thing that gets depleted. If time goes by and the person you care about doesn't seem to get better, you will start to doubt that your efforts are making a difference or that you are doing the right things. And from there you might start to doubt yourself in other things and begin to think you must be lacking in empathy, in wisdom, in competence, and other strengths.

Remind yourself that when someone is suffering from anxiety, progress can be very slow. There can be movement forward as well as steps backward. And much of the initial progress will be invisible, even to the person who is suffering. A glass of water filled drop by drop won't spill over the rim until it is so full that a single last drop breaks the surface tension and causes a gush of water to leave the glass. It takes a lot of drops of water in the form of security, the steadfast belief of friends and family, the staunch ongoing work of changing thinking habits, and the support of medical and mental health professionals before even the first outward changes in behavior can become visible. And there are many glasses to fill before the work will be done.

You need to remember that and have faith that what you are doing is making a positive difference. You also need to recognize that much of who you are, what you know, what you stand for, and what you are capable of, is invisible, too. Or at least not visible all the time. Certainly, not everyone you know knows everything about you. If asked, you, too, would be at a loss to describe all these things about yourself because they wouldn't occur to you or you might have trouble finding the words for them.

If you do become distraught and frustrated and start to attack yourself because you can't see the improvement that might actually be taking place very slowly day-to-day, then make a new list of your skills, talents, accomplishments, interests, positive acts, character traits, and inner resources, or ask some of your friends to name three things they like about you and something they think you are good at. This will help you maintain your inner strength, and help to sustain you as you join the person you care about in pushing back anxiety.

Afterword

This book isn't only about how to help someone in your life who is suffering from a form of anxiety. It is about easing your way as you channel time, energy, and love in her direction.

The suggestions in this book are just that—suggestions. As time goes on, you will find yourself tailoring your words to his situation, suiting your actions to her personality. This will begin to happen without conscious thought. You will have more confidence that the things you say and do are supportive, and you will feel more comfortable in your relationship. When anxiety no longer overshadows everything, when neither of you is concerned about putting a foot wrong, you will interact with one another in a natural way.

And that is what you want. When you interact in a natural way, you will each feel like peers in the relationship, as adults with competence, dignity, self-respect, and the respect of others. Maybe as coworkers who are each valued members of a team. Maybe as friends who enjoy each other's company and know they can share things and count on each other. Maybe both.

When we can feel this about ourselves and the people around us, and can feel this is how they feel about us, we can move forward, find strength and help, and get through the parts of life that are rough.

I hope this book can help you in that journey.

"*The problem of life is to change worry into thinking, and anxiety into creative action.*"

∽ HAROLD B. WALKER

Resources

༄

How to Learn More:
Finding Information and Support

Many people have been where you are now, and many of them have done what they could to make life easier for those who come after them. They've formed organizations to provide support, to educate, to lobby for research, to advocate for understanding, and to listen when you call and point you in the right direction. They've established centers for evaluation and treatment. If you are looking for a better understanding of what people with anxiety face, for ways to help, for people to talk to, for support groups, treatment options, referrals, the latest research, success stories, what to expect, where to go for screenings, treatment centers near you that specialize in anxiety disorders, books to consult or books and videos accessible to children, here are some places to start:

Screening for anxiety
National Anxiety Disorder Screening Project
Free screenings
For information call 888-442-2022 or check out their Web site ,
www.freedomfromfear.org.

Screening for depression
Screening for Mental Health
Phone: 781-239-0071
Web site: www.nmisp.org

Check the Web site for the nearest screening center and free screening dates.

Or check the Web site of the National Mental Health Association, www.nmha.org, for an online depression screening test.

ORGANIZATIONS THAT FOCUS ON ANXIETY

AGORAPHOBICS BUILDING INDEPENDENT LIVES (ABIL)
RICHMOND, VA
ABIL links individuals to support groups throughout the country and offers a message board so people can support each other online. It provides information and guidance on diagnosis, treatment, coping strategies, and everyday life to sufferers, family members, clinicians, and other mental health professionals through articles, book reviews, a quarterly newsletter, answers to commonly asked questions, support group meetings, and training of support group facilitators.

ANXIETY DISORDERS ASSOCIATION OF AMERICA
SILVER SPRING, MD
ADAA is dedicated to making people aware of the serious nature of anxiety disorders and how they affect people. It promotes research into their causes, the development of treatment options, and the dignity of the people who suffer from them. ADAA provides information to health professionals, educators, sufferers, their families, and legislators. Its members come from all these groups as well as researchers. In addition to general information, it helps individuals locate treatment centers and support groups and other resources that can help them. And it makes media kits available to local communities to promote understanding and reduce the stigma that some people associate with anxiety disorders.

NATIONAL CENTER FOR POST-TRAUMATIC STRESS DISORDER
The National Center for PTSD is a comprehensive research, information, evaluation, treatment, support, and training organization. Though originally established to support veterans, it now encompasses the full gamut

of PTSD and has become the national clearinghouse for information, current views, and treatment approaches. The center provides assessment instruments and treatment referrals. Their Web site includes fact sheets, a research quarterly, clinical quarterly, articles, frequently asked questions, and more. It also includes the PILOTS Database, an index to literature on the subject, which includes over twenty-two thousand abstracts. Some of the site is addressed to the lay person, some of it to clinicians.

OBSESSIVE-COMPULSIVE FOUNDATION (OCF)
NEW HAVEN, CT
OCF was founded by people with OCD to educate the public and keep professionals up-to-date, promote research into causes and treatments, and give assistance to people with OCD and their families. It offers numerous articles, access to support groups, an online bookstore, and a newsletter. OCF also maintains a list of treatment providers—mental health professionals who specialize in treating OCD in adults or have the subspeciality of treating children who have OCD. In addition to annual membership conferences, OCF directs The Behavior Therapy Institute (BTI), which trains mental health professionals in the latest treatment techniques. You can contact OCF for information via their Web site or by phone for information and referrals, or leave a message at any other time with your name and address, and an information packet and a referral list (for the state in which you live) will be mailed to you.

OTHER ORGANIZATIONS THAT CAN HELP

AMERICAN SELF-HELP GROUP CLEARINGHOUSE
Cedar Knolls, New Jersey

ASSOCIATION FOR ADVANCEMENT OF BEHAVIOR THERAPY
New York, New York

CHILD AND ADOLESCENT BIPOLAR FOUNDATION (CABF)
Wilmette, Illinois

DEPRESSION AND BIPOLAR SUPPORT ALLIANCE (DBSA)
(formerly known as the National Depressive and Manic-Depressive Association)
Chicago, Illinois

DEPRESSION AND RELATED AFFECTIVE DISORDERS ASSOCIATION (DRADA)
Baltimore, Maryland

NATIONAL ALLIANCE FOR THE MENTALLY ILL (NAMI)
Arlington, Virginia

NATIONAL MENTAL HEALTH ASSOCIATION (NMHA)
Alexandria, Virginia

NATIONAL MENTAL HEALTH CONSUMERS' SELF-HELP CLEARINGHOUSE
Philadelphia, Pennsylvania

A SAMPLING OF RESEARCH AND TREATMENT CENTERS—FROM COAST TO COAST

If none of these are close by, call the one nearest you anyway. The people there can answer questions and may be able to refer you to a center in your area. Some treat adults, some children, some both. Some are also research facilities, which means they have funding for clinical trials and can offer free treatment. Some avoid medications; some work with a combination of approaches.

ANXIETY AND PHOBIA TREATMENT CENTER AT
WHITE PLAINS HOSPITAL CENTER
White Plains, NY

CENTER FOR ANXIETY AND RELATED DISORDERS AT BOSTON UNIVERSITY
Boston, MA

DEPRESSION CENTER AT UNIVERSITY OF MICHIGAN
Ann Arbor, MI
(A focus on treating childhood and teenage anxiety to prevent onset of depression)

MARYLAND CENTER FOR ANXIETY DISORDERS
University of Maryland

THE ROSS CENTER FOR ANXIETY AND RELATED DISORDERS
Washington, D.C. metropolitan area

THE SHYNESS CLINIC
Palo Alto, CA

STRESS AND ANXIETY DISORDERS CLINIC (UNIVERSITY OF ILLINOIS)
Chicago, IL

BOOKS, VIDEOS, AUDIO

For Adults

Amen, Daniel G., M.D., and Lisa C. Routh, M.D. *Healing Anxiety and Depression.* New York: G. P. Putnam's Sons, 2003. Focuses on different ways anxiety and depression can present either separately or together, what brain imaging technologies show is happening in the brain, and the various ways biological, social, psychological, and interpersonal therapies can work to treat them.

Bassett, Lucinda. *From Panic to Power: Proven Techniques to Calm Your Anxieties, Conquer Your Fears, and Put You in Control of Your Life.* New York: Quill (HarperCollins), 1995, 2001. Very accessible book for the layperson. Based on personal experience as well as work with a treatment center. Focuses on personal account, changing how one thinks and responds, how to talk to oneself, and how to deal with fearful feelings, agoraphobia, avoidance behaviors, panic attacks, eating disorders, and breaking a cycle that disrupts one's life and leads to nonfunctioning.

Beck, Aaron T., M.D., and Gary Emery, Ph.D., with Ruth L. Greenberg, Ph.D. *Anxiety Disorders and Phobias: A Cognitive Perspective.* New York: Basic Books, 1985. Comprehensive and helpful book with a clinical focus.

Bourne, Edmund J., Ph.D. *The Anxiety & Phobia Workbook.* Oakland, CA: New Harbinger, 1990. Helpful exercises to do alone or with others. (One of a series of workbooks by different authors that address specific anxiety disorders such as shyness and social anxiety, obsessive-compulsive disorder, agoraphobia, etc.)

Bourne, Edmund J., Ph.D. *Beyond Anxiety and Phobia: A Step-by-Step Guide to Lifetime Recovery, 2001.* Talks to the whole person: simplifying, desensitizing, values, meaning, humor, belief systems, alternative therapies, diet, relaxation; personality issues, perfectionism, dependency, need for approval, fears, getting stuck.

Brantley, Jeffrey, M.D. *Calming Your Anxious Mind: How Mindfulness and Compassion Can Free You From Anxiety, Fear, and Panic.* Oakland, CA: New Harbinger, 2003. Targets chronic anxiety.

Cronkite, Kathy. *On the Edge of Darkness: Conversations About Conquering Depression.* New York: Dell, 1994. Inspiring accounts from a wealth of well-known people and others from many walks of life. A number of them talk about the impact of anxiety and how they deal with it.

Dumont, Raeann. *The Sky Is Falling: Understanding and Coping with Phobias, Panic, and Obsessive-Compulsive Disorders.* New York: W.W. Norton & Company, 1996. Focuses on specific situations, how to do exposure, how to provide support.

Gardner, James, M.D., and Arthur H. Bell, Ph.D. *Overcoming Anxiety, Panic, and Depression: New Ways to Regain Your Confidence.* Franklin

Lakes, NJ: Career Press, 2000. Includes a section on the use of herbs and supplements.

Gravitz, Herbert L., Ph.D. *Obsessive-Compulsive Disorder: New Help for the Family*. Santa Barbara, CA: Healing Visions Press, 1998. Mostly directed at someone who is struggling with OCD, this book answers a host of questions. It also discusses how to provide support without being abusive, without being abused yourself, and without creating dependency.

Grayson, Jonathan, Ph.D. *Freedom from Obsessive-Compulsive Disorder: A Personalized Recovery Program for Living with Uncertainty*. New York: Jeremy P. Tarcher (Penguin), 2003. Shows people how to break through the cycle.

Ingersoll, Barbara D., Ph.D., and Sam Goldstein, Ph.D. *Lonely, Sad and Angry: How to Help Your Unhappy Child*. Plantation, FL: Specialty Press, Inc., 2001. Discusses ways to help children and adolescents suffering from anxiety, depression, or both.

O'Conner, Richard, Ph.D. *Undoing Depression: What Therapy Doesn't Teach You and Medication Can't Give You*. New York: Berkley Books, 1997. Discusses various approaches and how they work singly and in combination. Also discusses ways of thinking that can make recovery more difficult and recurrence more likely.

Osborn, Ian, M.D. *Tormenting Thoughts and Secret Rituals: The Hidden Epidemic of Obsessive-Compulsive Disorder*. New York: Dell Publishing, 1998. An in-depth discussion of symptoms and coping strategies by a doctor who struggled with OCD in his own life.

Penzel, Fred, Ph.D. *Obsessive-Compulsive Disorders: A Complete Guide to Getting Well and Staying Well*. New York: Oxford University Press, 2000. A comprehensive guide to OCD in children as well as in adults; discusses help for families, medications; has a glossary of terms.

Peurifoy, Reneau A., M.A., M.F.C.C. *Anxiety, Phobias, & Panic: A Step-by-Step Program for Regaining Control of Your Life*. New York: Warner Books, 1988, 1995.

Peurifoy, Reneau A., M.A., M.F.C.C. *Overcoming Anxiety: From Short-Term Fixes to Long-Term Recovery*. New York: Henry Holt and Company (an Owl Book), 1997. Takes all areas of a person's life into consideration.

Rapee, Ronald M., editor, and Susan H. Spence, Ph.D., Vanessa Cobham, Ph.D., Ann Wignall, M. Psych. *Helping Your Anxious Child: A Step-by-Step Guide for Parents*. Oakland, CA: New Harbinger, 2000. Provides practical, concrete suggestions; exercises; and techniques for realistic thinking.

Ross, Jerilyn. *Triumph Over Fear: A Book of Hope and Help for People with Anxiety, Panic Attacks, and Phobias*. New York: Bantam, 1995.

Ross, Jerilyn. *Freedom from Anxiety*. Chicago: Nightingale-Conant. A self-help program for phobias, social anxiety, and panic disorder. Incorporates audio and video materials. Can be ordered through www.RossCenter.com.

Stein, Murray B., M.D., and John R. Walker, Ph.D. *Triumph Over Shyness: Conquering Shyness and Social Anxiety*. New York: McGraw-Hill (co-published with The Anxiety Disorders Association of America), 2002. Covers many aspects, including the challenge of dating.

Weekes, Claire. Pioneered books with focus on practical approach. Information on medications is outdated, but many find the rest of her suggestions very helpful. Three books: *Hope and Help for Your Nerves*; *Peace from Nervous Suffering*; and *Agoraphobia: Simple Effective Treatments*. Reissued by Bantam in the 1980s. Continues to be available.

Weekes, Claire. *Pass Through Panic: Freeing Yourself from Anxiety and Fear*. Portland, ME: AudioFile, 2001. Audio cassette, from a series of radio programs recorded in 1967.

Wilensky, Amy S. *Passing for Normal: A Memoir of Compulsion*. New York: Broadway Books, 1999. A story of how the author came to terms with the two intertwined disorders affecting her life: OCD and Tourette's syndrome. She discusses many incidents from childhood as well as both her denial and search for strategies in adulthood.

Zimbardo, Philip. *Shyness: What It Is, What to Do about It*. New York: Addison-Wesley, 1977.

For Kids

Hamilton, DeWitt. Illustrated by Gail Owens. *Sad Days, Glad Days: A Story about Depression*. Morton Grove, IL: Albert Whitman & Company, 1995. Read-aloud for ages four to seven; Read-on-their-own for ages eight to eleven.

Hipp, Earl. *Fighting Invisible Tigers: A Stress Management Guide for Teens*. Minneapolis: Free Spirit Publishing, 1995.

Niner, Holly L. Greg Swearingen, illustrator. *Mr. Worry: A Story about OCD*. Morton Grove, IL: Albert Whitman & Co., 2004. For grades two to five.

Simon, Norma. Joe Lasker, illustrator. *How Do I Feel?* Morton Grove, IL: Albert Whitman & Company, 1970. For ages four to seven.

WEB SITES

www.freedomfromfear.org
www.nimh.nih.gov (and click on the anxiety link)